7 DAY MANIFESTATION EXPERIMENT

How You Can Create

the Life of Your Dreams

Steve Martile

Visit the Official Website at: www.freedomeducation.ca

Printed in the United States of America

First Printing: September 2022

Freedom Education Publishing

ISBN: 978-0-9917820-0-0 (Paperback)
ISBN: 978-0-9917820-1-7 (Electronic Book)
ISBN: 978-0-9917820-2-4 (Audio)

This book may be purchased for educational, business or sales promotional use. Special discounts are available on quantity purchases. For more information, please call or write.

Telephone: 705-618-0302 - Email: steve@freedomeducation.ca

DISCLAIMER

While the author and publisher have strived to be as accurate and complete as possible in the creation of this book, readers are cautioned to rely on their own judgment about their individ-ual circumstances to act accordingly.

The author and publisher are providing this information on an educational basis and will not be liable for damages arising out of, or in connection with, the use of the content in this book. This is a comprehensive limitation of liability that applies to all damages of any kind, including (without limitation) compensatory; direct, indirect or direct, indirect or consequential damages; loss of data, income or profit; loss of or damage to property and claims of third parties.

While all attempts have been made to verify information provided in this publication, the author and publisher assumes no responsibility for errors, omissions, or contrary interpretation of the subject matter herein. Any perceived slights of specific persons, peoples, or organizations are unin tentional. This book details the author's own personal experiences and opinions.

You understand that this book is not intended as a substitute for consul-tation with a licensed profes-sional. In the event you use any of the in-formation in this book for yourself, which is your constitutional right, the author and publisher assume no responsibility for your actions or outcomes.

Contents

Introduction

Peter was a client of mine from the UK who found me through a blog post and my YouTube videos. He was a guitarist and we had been working together for a few months. As we approached the Christmas season, Peter was feeling overwhelmed financially and oscillating between panic and serenity. He complained there wasn't enough time to complete tasks and he just had too much going on for him to get more guitar students.

After digging a little deeper, I realized Peter was focusing too much on his outer world. He was giving too much attention and energy to his outward environment. By placing his attention outside of himself, he was reinforcing that very environment. It was no wonder he was not creating the life he wanted.

Imagine printing out your resume on a piece of paper, finding a mistake, and then whiting out the mistake on your printed copy. You wouldn't re-print your resume from the original digital version and expect to see the mistake magically disappear. In other words, you can't change the paper copy (3D world) by "whiting out" mistakes you've made in 3D physical reality. Change has to come from within.

Your attention creates your reality. You are constantly reinforcing whatever you put your attention on. When you focus on everything happening outside of you, you simply get more of the same showing up in your life. This is fine when it is stuff you want, but what about when it is not?

If you want to create something new, you must go inside and make changes at that level of reality. To demonstrate this, I decided to run an experiment with Peter. This experiment would renew his faith in the process of manifestation and his ability to create something from nothing.

Before we go any further, let's first define the term 'manifestation.' Manifestation is when you are focusing your thoughts (intent) and energy (emotions) upon your desired outcome so that it materializes in physical form.

As part of this experiment, I asked Peter to choose

three simple items he would like to see happen over the next 7 days - things he really wanted in his life. Here is what we came up with:

1. Get asked out for a beer at the local pub.
2. Have someone cook dinner for him.
3. Win the card game he plays every Thursday.

Then we went back to the basic principles of manifestation. I gave him specific instructions on how to attract what he wanted. I then charged Peter with testing out this theory over the next 7 days.

Here were his results:

1. The chair of a committee he was on asked if he wanted a pint at the pub.
2. The same night when he got home from the pub, his partner had prepared a delicious dinner.
3. He won the card game on Thursday. In fact, he consistently got good cards all night!

Amazingly, he manifested every single item on his list in just four days. By following this simple process, which I call "The 7 Day Manifestation Experiment,"

Peter changed his inner digital world to create real 3D world results.

7 Day Manifestation Experiment

I am living proof that these techniques work. I started as a mechanical engineer and then became a life coach. Today I run a marketing agency that helps entrepreneurs build their businesses. My YouTube channel has over 1.5 million views. The reason I wrote this book is to remind you that you are the co-creator of your world. I wanted to give you easy-to-follow tools to manifest the life of your dreams. You are the wizard. You are the magician. You are the painter. You are the Picasso of your life. It's all you.

The first time I shared this technique on my blog, I quickly had more than 300 comments. People from all around the world shared their intentions and results from their own 7-day manifestation experiments. Some people connected with long-lost friends, attracted unexpected money or new cars. One person even attracted a brand-new house.

"Okay, I swear that this website is magic! I can't remember exactly what time I posted although I know that it says 1:41 p.m. in the above. If this time is correct, then approximately an hour and 15 minutes later I got a call from my Realtor, stating that she had an investor interested in my house and wanted to schedule a viewing. I took my family out to eat so they could look and returned an hour later.

Today, my realtor called me to say that the investor is offering our full asking price for the house and we just have to see if the mortgage company accepts it, get my husband's credit score up a few points and get a new house.

DANG! That was quick!"

– Dianna

Two years after describing this technique on my blog, I decided to share the same process on my YouTube channel. Today that video has nearly half a million views and over 1,600 comments, again from people all around the world sharing their intentions being realized.

Here are a few more of those stories:

> "I am a musician, and I haven't had any gigs lately, and was in short of money. Honest to God, tonight I did this procedure for about an hour, practiced these affirmations, and just really believing that I'm doing great and having gigs...I REE-AALLY and truly believed it, without a doubt. Only a half an hour after I stopped the process, I received a phone call from a friend who owns a bar and was offered two months gigs scheduled over the summer until September, with 2 gigs per week! Needless to say, you bet I accepted it. I couldn't believe it. MANIFESTATION, IN JUST HALF AN HOUR. This, people, is the truth. I was flabbergasted."
>
> – Meho M.

"OMG! I decided to do this experiment, and I chose to have some money come to me, unexpectedly, just enough to allow me to buy a particular thing I wanted, (but thought I shouldn't waste money on). My week ended a few days ago, and it appeared it hadn't worked. Then today I decided to chase up on an email I received last week, which I thought was a scam, but wanted to be sure. It said it was from the electricity supply company I used 3 years ago, saying I had a credit on my account. For 1, it's not like me to have credit on an account and forget! 2. Why are they chasing me about it three years later? 3. I was sure it was a scam. Anyway, just to be sure and check if it was a scam, I rang the company. They told me I do have credit and will be sending me a refund. The amount is just over the price of the item I was doing this experiment on!!! Thank you, Universe!!"

– Christine W.

The techniques in this book are based on the premise that everything is energy, and everything is connected. Our observation of reality is what creates our reality. You can influence your perception and your universe – and you do that with your thoughts and feelings. The bottom line is that *you* create your world. But it's not something you do alone. It's a partnership where you walk hand in hand with the Creator. You partner with the Creator to change your reality.

Creator, you say? Imagine the Creator not as one God or ruler or supreme being. Rather, the Creator is the benevolent energy that supports all of life. The Creator is God manifested through the human that uses intent. We all have access to this energy. We all have the ability to connect with the benevolent energy that supports all of life to create what we want.

The issue for so many people is that they get 'caught up' in focusing on their external realities. When this happens, we just reproduce more of what already is. What we forget is that when we focus on everything that is happening outside of us, we get more of those items showing up in our life. The good news is that we have the power to interrupt this cycle. We can break the pattern.

What you'll learn in this book is how to:

- Develop empowering self-confidence.

- Use your imagination to attract miracles into your life.

- Train yourself to focus on your 'inner being' and nourish the connection with the benevolent loving energy of the Creator.

- Set deep level intentions to reprogram your subconscious mind and realize your full potential.

- Overcome limiting beliefs that prevent you from attracting the abundance and joy you deserve.

- Use the illusion of truth to train your mind to focus your thoughts upon a desired outcome so that it materializes in physical form.

I'm thrilled you are reading this book, and I'm excited to show you what is possible for your life. Regardless of what has happened to you in the past, you have the ability to live an extraordinarily abundant life.

Sit back, relax, and enjoy the ride!

Chapter 1

What Super Nintendo Taught Me About Manifesting

"It's a funny thing about life, if you refuse to accept anything but the best, you very often get it."

– John Kehoe,
Quantum Warrior:
The Future of the Mind

Most people wouldn't expect the same personality who does engineering to also be a life coach. So how did I go from engineer to life coach?

I've had some defining moments along my journey. They always came with a fair amount of discomfort. One of those moments occurred while I was working in Toronto as an HVAC engineer. One weekend my wife and I were driving north to Sudbury in our Honda

Accord to see family. We were talking about the new job I had started six months earlier.

I remember saying to her, "I feel depressed."

My wife says, "Is it me?"

"No, of course it's not you," I said. "It's the work I'm doing."

I felt this rigid programming take over when I was in my job. It was as if there were two of me. One part of me felt that I should keep everyone happy. Keep the peace. Don't ruffle any feathers. Don't rock the boat. Don't do anything that will upset anyone. Don't stand up for yourself, especially if it might upset someone else. We wouldn't want that.

The other part of me (the real me) was screaming inside to do the things that made me feel happy, to be true to myself, to honor my feelings. I needed to speak up for myself at meetings when I felt guided to do that. I needed to explore, to be creative, to try new things, to be less rigid and more adventurous.

The real me was getting louder and louder. I knew I needed to make a change, but the truth was I felt trapped. One part of me had taken the job in Toronto because it was the 'right thing to do' and the 'money was good.' Yet the real me was pushing to emerge. It wouldn't stand down.

I started working on projects for two different senior engineers. They both had conflicting ideas about which projects were the most important. Imagine walking into a meeting where you're told that project X needs to be your highest priority. You leave that meeting and walk into another meeting five minutes later, and you're told by a totally different supervisor that project Y is more important than project X.

It was driving me nuts. I was pulling my hair out because I wanted both supervisors to be happy with me. I had the so-called "disease to please". I was miserable. Pleasing others was a trap I had created for myself. I desperately wanted out.

That's when I started looking for answers. I decided to open my mind to new ideas. I decided I was going to do something different because the pain and internal discomfort were too much to bear. I had to change course, so I started reading books and becoming more receptive to new ideas.

One of the first books I read was *Think and Grow Rich*. Written by a guy named Napoleon Hill in 1937 at the height of the Great Depression, the book has sold over 15 million copies. It blew the limitations on my mind wide open. The idea that you could 'think' and grow rich was revolutionary for me.

The second book I read was Tony Robbins' *Unlimited Power*. Robbins describes how he helped top performers achieve at their highest level and how readers can use the same techniques to accomplish their own goals. Both of these books expanded my mind. I could identify with what the authors were saying. It was all about empowering yourself, feeling empowered, and being self-reliant. It was about doing things that made you feel happy and fulfilled. I desperately needed to hear this message. It was a lifeline.

As I was reading these books and others like them, I started making different decisions. My perception changed and I came to a new understanding that I could think and become rich. Gradually, I began to invest in live training and meeting other people who were on a similar journey.

The first personal development course I took was in February 2006 in Toronto. It was a training course that involved coaching. We participated in a large group of around 100 people once per week and then had a smaller group of six members where we did the coaching, led by one coach.

During the second week of this course, the leader of our group quit. She just left with no warning. Now there were five of us left. Everyone looked around and asked, "Who's going to be the leader now?" Without hesitation, I raised my hand and said, "I'll do it!" I was starting to speak up for myself and follow my inner guidance. It felt good, but I didn't care about being the leader for the sake of being the leader. I raised my hand because I wanted to do the coaching.

That's when my life really started to change. Coaching was a Godsend. I loved coaching. It was better than breathing. It made me feel alive. I got to help people and change lives. My outlook on life was becoming very different. As I was coaching and going through these changes, I ran into the best man at my wedding. "You're a totally different person," he remarked.

I was happy and the difference was noticeable. I realized that we're all happier when we are actively pursuing our potential. We don't want to be locked into a room or an office or a cubicle and left for dead. We want to truly experience life. The way we do this is through our own growth.

My energy had changed when I got into coaching. Like many coaches do in the very beginning, I started off doing it for free. I loved it. Coaching was giving me life and a renewed sense of purpose. I kept coaching while I was working at my full-time job. It was now 2008, right around the time of the great financial crisis.

By this time, I had been working at my engineering company for five years. All the while, I was attending more seminars, reading more self-help books, and generally meeting more and more people who were like me – human beings who believed we had more potential.

During one of those seminars, I got this wild idea: *What if I quit my job and started a coaching business?* It didn't take long for this to become more than just an idea. In the fall of November 2009, I quit my job. My wife thought I had gone off the deep end. We had a mortgage and bills to pay. But I was convinced I could do this.

Dennis was the president of the engineering company at the time. I still remember the day I walked into his office. It was a small company with around 200 employees and Dennis always had an open-door policy. I walked right into his office and asked him if he had a few minutes to chat. I told him I was going to leave to start this coaching business. He walked right up to me and gave me a big hug and congratulated me.

That was unexpected! He must have somehow picked up on my enthusiasm. Dennis told me that I could work on contract with the company during my transition. That would give me a chance to put some money aside instead of going cold turkey and diving right into my coaching business.

Wow!

If I was going to work on contract, then that meant I was going to be hired as an engineering consultant. After meeting with Dennis, I did some homework to see what engineering consultants were getting paid in Ontario based on the PEO (Professional Engineers of

Ontario) Fee Guide.

I discovered I could charge $120 per hour as an engineering consultant. That was quite eye opening. Based on the projects I had up to that point, I estimated it would take about 4 months (at 20 hours per week) to finish all the projects I had been working on for the company.

If I committed 20 hours a week, at $120 an hour, that would be almost $10,000 a month, which was double what I was making from my job! "Holy cow," I thought. "This is good money."

Now that I had a rough plan, I developed an outline of what I was going to do, the projects I was going to work on and how it was going to benefit the company. I figured four months to finish all these projects on contract gave me plenty of time to start making money in my new coaching business.

I pitched the idea to the VP of Operations. He agreed, and I sent him my proposal with my engineering consulting fees. The fees were added to the company's budget, and I was approved almost right away to start working on contract as a consultant. A few weeks later I started receiving those checks for $10,000.

I was thrilled. I knew I had *created* this and was living out my potential. Life was great!

Unfortunately, I soon began to feel that I wasn't worthy of the money. It was too easy, and I felt that I was getting paid too much. That's when the self-sabotage patterns started to show up.

One afternoon - about eight weeks after I started working on contract - I remember the CFO saw me talking on the phone outside of work. Our eyes made contact and I felt this strange panic inside. I knew something was wrong.

Two weeks later I was told that my contract was going to end. Most of the projects had been finished and other managers on staff had been assigned to the tasks I was working on. I was going to get my last paycheck in January 2010. After that, I was on my own.

The reason I panicked was because I still hadn't figured out how to make money in my coaching business. I had a lot of doubts about making real money as a coach. In fact, I didn't make very much money at all. I was basically self-employed with no income.

However, I learned a lot from that experience. You've got to pick things that are believable to you if you want to create them in your own reality. That's how the muscle grows.

Later that year things were looking up. I was doing some of my best writing that year and doing a bit of coaching as well. But I wasn't bringing in the kind of money that I had before, which wasn't' helping the relationship with my wife.

My wife was concerned because we were spending twice as much as we were earning every month. Our credit lines were getting exhausted, and we were going into more debt. Looking back, I still don't blame her for being upset with me at the time.

Around mid-summer of 2010, I finally sat down to look at our bank statements. That's when I realized I needed to get another job.

By this point, I had internalized this idea that the Universe or this field of intention will give me what I want. It had worked pretty well so far, aside from a bit of financial debt. But I just knew I could make money in a stable job.

The big difference was that I wanted to find a job that would make me happy, not miserable.   So that's what I set out to do.

Every day I started to visualize doing work that would make me happy. In the beginning, not much happened. I was just happy and broke. Each morning, I woke up feeling enthusiastic and excited thinking about working in this imaginary job that would give me joy.

But then in October of that year around the Canadian Thanksgiving, something miraculous happened. I got a surprise call from a recruiter for an interview with an engineering firm. Five days later I received an email with my first job offer plus a $10,000 relocation bonus.

Now keep in mind, this was during the financial crisis, so there weren't a lot of good jobs, but I managed to find one. Not only that – I found a job that made me happy.

I remember during the initial interview with the owner of this engineering firm, he asked me, "Do you do any sales?"

I said, "No, but I would love to learn." That job was

my introduction to sales. I learned a lot from my boss and from being in that job, but more importantly I also learned that I'm the one who created this opportunity.

I put intention behind this, and it showed up. I created it. I'll never forget that.

A lot of people hear my story, and say "What you're talking about, I've heard about this, it's the secret. It's the law of attraction. I tried it, and it didn't work."

So how do you make it work?

For now, I'll explain how I came to this realization, the idea that 'you create your world,' and then I'll dive deeper into how this works because this concept came to me slowly over time. It didn't happen overnight.

One of the first times I remember intentionally sitting down to manifest something was when I was in my early thirties, playing Super Nintendo with the best man from my wedding.

The Super Nintendo Experience

It was a Thursday in June. My wife had bought a couple of bags of chips and a dozen old Milwaukee beers. My best man Kris and I decided to get together to play some video games. We would get together every so often to play the classic games on Super Nintendo.

NHL 95 was one of our favorites. On this particular night, my buddy Kris was beating me badly every single game. I couldn't seem to score a goal. He kept winning game after game.

This went on for about two hours. We're having a couple of beers, playing NHL 95, and he takes a break to go to the bathroom.

Now I was familiar with this idea of intention, and I had read a lot of books on it up to this point, maybe 400 or so books, mostly on spirituality and personal development. I had this intuitive sense for it - the idea that we create our world.

When my friend went to the bathroom, I just sat there, closed my eyes, and visualized scoring goals. I visualized how it would feel. It's not like I had never scored goals before, so I already knew what it would feel like – it was familiar to me.

I took a few moments to myself and just sat there with my eyes closed seeing myself scoring goals and winning the game. I even heard my friend getting angry and swearing at me for starting to score, what he would say and then laughing about it. It was a game after all.

Once I'd gone into this meditative state for 2-3 minutes, I felt a lot more relaxed and playful. Earlier I'd had anxiety about our game because I kept losing.

When my friend came back from the washroom, we started to play again. I scored the first goal. A few minutes later, I scored the second goal. My friend scored a goal and then I scored a third goal. My friend starts swearing at me just as I had visualized. I start laughing. He can't believe his change in luck and that I am winning for once – and I just kept laughing, being playful and having fun. I won the game.

That experience reminded me of how we can create things, have fun and just be ourselves. It also reminded me of this quote from W. Clement Stone: "Big doors swing on little hinges." Meaning that by focusing on the things we want, we bring them into being without effort. That our focus can move mountains when applied the right way. I felt like I had just grasped what that little hinge was.

I'll never forget that moment and what I learned that day: *we create our reality.* That's how it all started. That experience led me to set bigger intentions. I realized that all we need to do is relax and imagine the future we want.

As we go deeper down the rabbit hole, I'm going to show you how to bend reality using intention. Before we do that, it's important that you have a broader understanding of how the Universe works, how we are all connected, and how we communicate with the invisible world around us.

Chapter #2

Everything is Energy

"Everything is energy and that's all there is to it. Match the frequency of the reality you want and you cannot help but get that reality. It can be no other way. This is not philosophy. This is physics."

– Darryl Anka

During my final years working as an engineer, I worked in jobs and around people who were just negative. I interviewed with the owner of this one company and during the interview, the owner said to me, "I hope you stay with us." That was an interesting thing to say in the first interview, I thought but, we had a mortgage and bills to pay, and I was in between jobs and desperate, so I took the job anyway. I needed money coming in right away.

On Monday afternoon of my first week of work with

this new company, the owner had a temper tantrum. During a conference call he started yelling at the person on the phone and throwing erasers and pens across the room.

The next morning, the owner was in a good mood. He saw me in the office and gave me a high give. This guy's a nut-job I thought. His emotions are all over the place. One minute he's your best friend, and an hour later he's at a war with you. After a couple days of working there I noticed he would yell at his employees regularly too. As I was working very closely with him, this really made me reconsider working there.

By Thursday of the next week, I had reached my tipping point. The owner was on a construction site, and he phoned me about an estimate from a concrete supplier. He said, "Did you get the estimate?" and when I replied "No" he lost it. He started swearing in Italian and going off the handle. This guy is crazy, I thought. I'm thinking, that's it! I'm out of here! Later that evening I wrote my resignation letter.

The very next day I had my letter of resignation in

hand and ready to go. I walked straight up to the Human Resources Manager and gave her my letter, the keys to the brand-new pickup truck they'd bought me, the laptop they'd given me and the phone, and said, "it's just not working out." The Manager said, "Is it him? Is it because of the owner?" And I'm like, "yup, it's him."

As I was leaving the office, a project administrator I had been working with came up to me and said, "I can't believe you're doing this. I would leave, but I have rent and bills to pay. Good for you." That's when I told her, "Nobody deserves to be treated this way. Besides, I know I can find somewhere else to work that appreciates and values the work I do." She gave me a big hug, and I left the office. I drove off with no job prospects and a ton of bills to pay but feeling like a million bucks! I had this huge sense of relief like a weight had been lifted from my shoulders.

As an engineer, I worked in places with negative vibrations that would affect my state of being. Because of that, I had to learn ways to not only protect myself, but also how to avoid these types of people, and set boundaries.

What I also found in my experience working with other people is that you don't necessarily have to be around these people physically for them to affect you. You can be on the phone with them, on another continent, or even just texting them. You can be thousands of miles away and still be affected by their energy.

So that got me curious about how this all worked.

Were we really all connected? Was there really a 'field of intention' that preceded the creation of all forms of matter?

Quantum Entanglement

Everything's energy, and everything's connected. All around us and within us there is a field of intention that you can influence to create your world.

The concept of quantum entanglement provides us with some clues. This theory in quantum mechanics states that when you do something to one of a pair of entangled particles, it instantly affects the properties of the other, no matter how far away the other is.

This connection at a distance is what Einstein referred to as "spooky action at a distance." Known in quantum physics as non-local communication, it basically means that we are constantly communicating through this 'field of intention' with all matter non-locally. Quantum entanglement collapses all physical reality into a single reality, meaning there is no separation between objects – it's all one reality.

"The new biology reveals that the invisible forces that we collectively refer to as mind, form a field which shape our biology."

– Dr. Bruce Lipton,
The Biology of Belief

An example of this is when your vibration entangles with another person's vibration. What results is a new frequency or energetic state. Let's say you go through your meditation, you do your affirmations, and you start your day feeling great. You could generally be a happy person, but as soon as you 'bump into' someone who's in a generally negative state (lower vibration) your energy becomes entangled with that person.

That entanglement leaves you feeling a little less than joyful. You might begin to have negative thoughts or start worrying about something that hasn't bothered you for weeks or even years. This is entanglement in action.

Once you entangle your vibration with someone else, you either 'pick up' on the energy of that lower vibration (which can bring you down) or they pick up on your higher vibration (making them generally feel better, or even inspired).

Here's the general rule: the degree of the intensity of the higher of the two vibrations will always win. This means that the energy that's more intense (either positive or negative) becomes the more dominant vibration.

Your vibration is what creates your reality. There are trillions of cells in your body that oscillate, and that vibration emits a frequency.

"Quantum physicists discovered that physical atoms are made up of vortices of energy that are constantly spinning and vibrating; each atom is like a wobbly spinning top that radiates energy.

– Dr. Bruce Lipton,
The Biology of Belief

The possibilities, the opportunities, and the paths that shows up in your life are always driven by these frequencies and vibrations. This field is what precedes matter. Change the field, and you change the matter.

Here's another way to look at this. Let's say you're having a great day – it might be Friday and you're excited about the weekend. Because you're generally feeling good, you could say that you're at a frequency vibration of 5Hz (the number is arbitrary, but the concept is what matters most).

Later that day, you decide to meet with a friend at a coffee shop who's in a denser vibration of say 2Hz. They are in a complaining mode and even a bit angry at the world and they want to tell you all about it.

If the intensity of the lower vibration (2Hz) of your

friend is higher than your positive vibration (5Hz), once you 'entangle' with them, your energetic state is going to change. You 'pick up' on their vibration and feelings and when you walk out of that coffee shop, you're going to feel like a different person. Maybe now you're at 3Hz because your frequency has dropped. You don't feel as inspired as you did before you met with your friend. You've completely shifted into a lower vibration. You can feel the difference.

So, what can we do in these situations?

The first thing is to realize that quantum entanglement is a real phenomenon. You are constantly shifting and changing your vibration based on the people you surround yourself with and with the places you go.

The second thing is to embrace that all people are different. Some people are just angry at the world. Some people don't want to change. That's ok. Don't try to change them. Just let them be. The more you try to change them, the angrier they get. They might not even know what to do if they didn't have something to complain about. Let them be – its' not your job to change them.

No doubt you've met people like this. Years ago, in my twenties I had a buddy who would always call me and complain about his girlfriend. There was constantly something new for him to complain about. If it wasn't his girlfriend, he would call to complain about his job. Finally, one day I said to him, "Dude, if you keep calling me and complaining every time you call, I'm not going to want to talk with you anymore. Why don't you call and tell me about what's working in your life?"

Guess what? He literally stopped calling me. I wasn't going to put up with his negativity anymore, and he wasn't ready to change. He got it, and that was that. After that we kind of just went our separate ways.

But it's not just with other people. We get entangled with places too.

I love the beach and the sun. Every time I go to the ocean, I get into this very deeply relaxed state. When we were living in Florida last year, my wife and I would go to the beach to chill out and enjoy nature, the dolphins, the turtles, the birds, and the seemingly endless ocean. If I had any stress or was worried about something, then without fail going to the beach just melted all those feelings away.

I'm sure you have places where you feel that, too. That's quantum entanglement in action. You're literally entangling with the energy of a given place. Maybe you like to hike in nature because it makes you feel at peace. You're picking up on the vibrations of that place. You feel the difference on a cellular level.

The Field in Nature

It's not just feelings you get, it's new information as well. One of my favorite illustrations of quantum entanglement is from the sea turtle episode in the "Planet Earth" documentary series.

The sea turtle is born on a beach on the coast of India and leaves to travel thousands of miles across the ocean. Many years later when the sea turtle is an adult and looking for a place to lay her eggs, she returns to the exact same beach, in the exact same spot where she was born to nest her eggs.

Her 'inner compass' that guided her back to her place of birth is another form of quantum entanglement. This is because there is an exchange of information that is invisible – that "spooky action at a distance" that Einstein spoke about. It's as if mother earth is secretly whispering *"go this way"* to the sea turtle.

That's what I mean when I say, "everything is connected." Once you realize that you're connected to all places and all people by some hidden quantum force, you begin to value and set boundaries of what you will and won't accept in your environment.

How We Influence Matter

Science also shows us how we are connected on a fundamental level and how our emotions influence objects non-locally. When I say non-locally, I mean that we influence material reality outside of our bodies. The documentary *"I Am"* directed by Tom Shadyac (who also directed Ace Ventura with Jim Carey) illustrates this effect.

During the documentary, Tom is wired with electrodes. The electrodes measure different voltages while the interviewer asks Tom some provocative questions. When asked about his relationship with his lawyer, Tom immediately responds with a strong emotion. (Not surprisingly, it turns out Tom has a bad relationship with his lawyer).

The electrodes respond with jumps in voltage in response to Tom's emotions. But what's really wild is that a few feet in front of him is a cup of yogurt that has electrodes in it as well. Those electrodes were also tied to a meter. Any time Tom was asked a specific question about his lawyer or any other question that evoked these strong emotions, the yogurt likewise 'reacted' with high spikes in voltage.

The fact that an organic material like yogurt can 'pick up' on our emotions is quite exciting. It means that we are literally affecting the world around us with our emotions.

Phenomena like this are rarely explained by the physics you learned in high school. In fact, there were only two pages on quantum physics in my high school physics textbook. There is so much more to this 'field of intention' that we currently don't understand.

Quantum Physics Secrets

The double slit experiment is a famous physics demonstration of the connection between mind and matter. This experiment was first performed by Thomas Young in 1802 as a demonstration of the wave behavior of light. It was later extended to include atoms and molecules.

The basic premise of the experiment is that matter can behave as both particles and waves. A particle can be a molecule, an atom, or the nucleus of an atom. These are all particles and the building blocks of nature. Particles can come together and behave as a wave. Some examples of a wave could be light, EMF's or sound waves.

During the experiment, electrons would switch from waves into particles instantly, but only when scientists were observing them. When the observation device was switched off the result changed. The particles began behaving as waves.

Were the electrons 'aware' that someone was watching them? It certainly appeared so. This experiment has been verified countless times with the same consistent outcome: particles change their behaviour when we observe them. The electrons acted differently when they were being watched.

This has been referred to in quantum physics as the 'observer effect.'

"In atomic physics, we can never speak about nature without, at the same time, speaking about ourselves."

– Frijitov Capra,
Austrian-born American physicist

This creates some huge implications. You see, all matter is composed of these tiny electrons or particles. These particles are everywhere – they are the building blocks of the universe. They are the foundation to your physical body, the house you live in, the car you drive, and the money in your bank account.

Our entire reality is filled with these tiny particles. And these particles respond to the way we observe them. That's right - we influence the cosmic waves of matter simply by observing. In other words, our observation of reality is what *creates* our reality.

Our observation is where we place our attention. Based on the consistent findings of the double slit experiment it's clear that our attention influences the behaviour of very tiny particles. Since all matter is made of these tiny particles, we could also say that the behaviour of matter is influenced by our observation.

Put another way, your attention is what holds your world together. Your attention is what creates your physical reality. This means that everything you observe has originated from thought, intentionally or unintentionally, consciously, or unconsciously. That's why it is so important to become aware of what you're thinking and to direct those thoughts so that you are only thinking about what you want to see show up in your life.

Your thoughts are at the source of your current reality. If you're not happy with your current results, then start to create new thoughts. Create a new picture, a new image of reality so that the quantum world can work its magic.

"It is a single cell's 'awareness' of the environment that primarily sets into motion the mechanisms of life."

– Bruce H. Lipton,
The Biology of Belief

Fields of Possibility

In 1942, Harold Saxton Burr, professor of anatomy at Yale University School of Medicine, was one of the first people to measure what he called "bio-fields" in living things. Burr was fascinated by this invisible realm of energy. He studied cancer in mice by taking voltage measurements on and outside of the bodies of these mice. As he was measuring these fields, he established a baseline voltage for a healthy mouse.

After a few months of these measurements, Burr noticed a significant increase above the baseline voltage. Initially he had no explanation for the mysterious jump in voltage but what he discovered next was astonishing.

Ten to fourteen days after this spike in voltage appeared, Burr discovered and diagnosed these mice with cancer. It appeared the field that was measured had increased at least 10 days *prior* to the physical manifestation of the disease. The results were consistent with 95% of the mice in his test group.

Burr's initial work in the measurement of EMFs (Electromagnetic fields) on mice indicated that the field preceded biology. It confirmed that matter was in fact generated by this field. Here's a snippet of an interview with Dr. Joe Dispenza as he discusses Burr's earlier studies on uterine cancer in women:

"Every single woman that had a pattern in the field (that he measured), had a pattern in the physical body of cancer. But there was a certain percentage (of women) that had some (pattern) in the field but didn't have the cancer in the body.... yet! But they ultimately developed the cancer.

He (Burr) was looking at matter thinking, there's a

glow and that matter is emitting a field. But that's not the case. The field is creating matter. **Change the field, and you change matter.**"

Once you change the field, you change matter. This invisible field of intention has been called many things over the years: the etheric field, the ether, plasma, the mind of God, or infinite intelligence. Regardless of what you call it, the field of intention exists for your benefit.

In *The Holographic Universe* Michael Talbot explains what is possible with this field of intention:

"Remote viewing experiments have shown that people can accurately describe distant locations even when there are no human observers present at the locations. Similarly, subjects can identify the contents of a sealed box randomly selected from a group of sealed boxes and whose contents are therefore completely unknown. This means that we can do more than just tap into the senses of other people. We can also tap into reality itself to gain information. As bizarre as this sounds, it is not so strange when one remembers that in a holographic universe, consciousness pervades all matter, and "meaning" has an active presence in both the mental and physical worlds."

Your body is composed of tiny particles that vibrate and oscillate. These spinning particles act as matter or waves depending on if they are being watched by an observer or not. When these particles are watched by an observer, they behave differently - they act as waves. As you become the observer of our experience, you become a wave of possibilities. As you change the way you look at things, the things you look at change.

With this basic understanding of how all things are connected, you can now experiment with different ways to change the field and therefore change matter. This experiment will give you some structure on how to focus to influence your physical reality. That's where we are going next.

Chapter 3

Manifesting, Where to Start?

> *"All life is an experiment.*
> *The more experiments you make the better."*
>
> – Ralph Waldo Emerson

It was about three weeks before my wife and I were about to leave Idaho to drive back to Canada. Money had been really tight for the previous few weeks because I hadn't had a new sale in over 8 weeks. I'd also had two clients ask me for a refund, which put our bank accounts in the negative.

We needed some money quick. Our credit cards were maxed out, and our savings was almost depleted. We weren't even sure if we had enough money to buy food or gas for the trip home! Things were not looking good.

I had done a quick look through our finances and realized I needed to come up with around $15,000 just to keep afloat and take care of our basic necessities.

So, I put together a plan with my wife as we had decided that if I couldn't find a way to come up with around $15,000 within the next 30 days, that I'd have to declare bankruptcy. Obviously, I didn't want to do that but I told her, "Give me 30 days, by then we'll be back in Canada. If I haven't made at least $15k by the time we get home, then I will drop this business completely. I will go back and get a job." That's the promise that I made to her, and then I got to work.

I was intentional with my actions and my meditations. I knew how to make money because I had been running this business for two years. It was just that I now had a firm deadline and I needed the money quick.

Three weeks went by and still no sales, but I was optimistic because I had two sales calls scheduled during the week that we were planning to drive back to Canada. I held those two sales calls on the road in the hotels we were staying in. Both of those sales closed, and the third client promised me the money once we were back in Canada. Two days after we drove across the Canadian/USA border I had $14,782 in my business account!

Your mind can bend reality. Your thoughts can create a new reality. But now I want you to prove that to yourself. Many doubters will say, "I've heard of the law of attraction, but that stuff doesn't work." This experiment is not for those non-believers. If you want this process to work for you then you must be open to new ideas and new information – you must be receptive to taking on new beliefs.

Now in this current moment, you're in one of two places. You either have what you want, and you recognize that you are good at manifesting and want to create more of what you want, or you feel that you are 'wanting' and 'needing' something to happen for you.

If you are 'needing' or 'wanting' something to happen, you will give off the experience and feeling (vibration) that you don't have what you want. This creates more scarcity and lack in your life.

In this chapter, I'm going to walk you through a simple process to create something new over the next 7 days. If you follow through with these steps, you might just surprise yourself. It's literally how you create your world. Remember, everything's energy, and everything's connected. There is this field of intention that you can influence to create your world.

I'm not asking you to adopt a new religion. I'm not trying to get you to do anything you don't want to do. You have free will. Think of this process like a new pair of jeans.

If you try on a pair of jeans and you like the way they feel, keep wearing them. If you try on the jeans and they feel too tight or they're not the right length, just take them off. Just make sure to put something else back on because no one wants to see you running around in your underwear!

This next part is important. If you want to play this cosmic game to the best of your ability, you'll need to ignore your attachment to your physical reality. Anything external to what's inside of your thoughts, your feelings, and your emotions is not your concern. What happens on the outside is always a surprise.

There is a field of intention that aligns with your inner being. When you align your inner being with this field, your physical reality changes. It's important to give this 'inner being' your ultimate focus. You're in complete control of this inner space. You control your thoughts and feelings. You have the willpower to focus on what you desire. You have control over your imagination, what you dream about and what you think about. You have control over your ability to act and to do the things that you need to do.

If you treat your world like that – a playground where you are focused on your inner being and not on the outside, not only will you be happier, but you'll also attract amazing things into your life without having to try so hard. When you realize that your sphere of influence is that inner space, it takes the pressure off. Life gets easy and you begin to have a lot more fun.

Instead of focusing on the physical outer world, focus on your avatar, your physical body and what you feel, not the game environment. The game environment is like the background in the Nintendo game I was playing with my best man. The game environment is your outer physical reality. It's the manifestation of a physical result. It's not the ultimate reality, but a holographic projection of what has been created in the field.

Remember, you are playing a game. The meat suit you call your body is just an avatar created in your physical game environment. When you change the field, you change matter. The game environment will change once your avatar in the game changes.

For example, instead of trying to get into a relationship with the person you think you need to be with, let the Creator decide that for you. Focus on what it would feel like to be with the person that brings you joy – what makes you happy – but don't obsess over a specific person. Let It be a surprise.

Mastering this process of manifestation requires you to train yourself to focus on your inner being, to focus on your desires, your feelings, and your vibration. Once you make that connection, oftentimes you get something 10 times better.

It's physics.

You might have a piece of business or a new client

that you're waiting on right now to send you money. You might have money waiting to come to you and it's not happening as fast as you would like.

The big question is why?

It's because you're distancing yourself from that money coming to you. You're interfering with it based on what you are thinking about, and that has created this distance, this gap between you and the money.

How do you do that?

Focusing on too much of the *how* will do it. Focusing on too much of the *when* will do it. Focus on too much of the *when* and *how* will definitely do it. The secret is changing the way you feel (your vibration) and what you think about.

Again, the doubters will say, "I expect money, but that's because I work as a sales rep. I know money is coming to me because I work in sales. I expect sales, and that's how I make my money."

Of course, that's how you make your money. The question is...does the money come from your circumstances or your expectation (how you feel about money)?

Deep down, you know this, and you know that if you can manage your expectations, you can create your own circumstances. But you must test this in your own experience.

Remember my Nintendo story from the first chapter? I'm playing video games with my friend and boom, I start winning. I start beating him. He was so shocked because the tide had changed very quickly in my favor. The energy shifted and so did the results. I figured that if this worked for Nintendo games, it probably works for money too.

In the beginning it was small amounts: $5, then $10, then $100. Now I'm doing it with tens of thousands of dollars, but it didn't happen overnight. It took years of practice. You are causing and creating everything in your life. You're causing the struggle, but you're also creating the bliss. When it comes to money, you're co-creating with the Creator, because everything is energy.

The idea is that you want to change your energy every day just by a little bit, and over the longer term, this energy change has a bigger impact on your results, your experience and what you attract.

Here's the 3-step process:

Step #1: Write down a list of 3 things you desire.

Get a piece of paper right now and start to write down a list. What are three things you desire to see happen over the next seven days?

One of them can be money. Let's say you have a new client about to sign up with you, and you know that you're going to get $5,000 from that sale, but you haven't yet. Write that down.

Here's what I want you to do next. Rate the believability of that intention happening on a 1-10 scale:

- 10, you absolutely believe it will show up and,
- 1, you don't believe it at all.

If you have a $5,000 sale coming to you, and on that 1-10 scale you believe the likelihood of that sale closing is a 1/10, then there's no way in hell it will show up. However, if you know the $5,000 sale is more likely and it's a 7 out of 10, then you're getting much warmer. You're getting closer to the sweet spot.

You want to set intentions based on what you believe will work. If it's too high and out of reach for your belief system, then you'll be disappointed. But if you pick something that is an 8/10 or higher, then you're right in the sweet spot. You can start to build that manifesting muscle.

As an example, if I know I have $3,000 coming to me because a client has verbally confirmed that they want to start in two weeks, then that is an 8/10 for me. I don't have the money yet, but I know it's coming.

You want to be an eight, nine or even a 10 on your believability scale so that you will attract the money you want. That's the key - it's got to be believable to *you*. That's where the magic happens. Your mind is elastic. It can expand and grow. And when you keep using this process, for seven days, for 21 days, 30 days, or even the next year, your level of believability will go up.

Instead of attracting $100 next year, it could be $1,000 because what you believe has increased over time. However, you first have to start with something that is believable to you. That's the first step. Write down a list of three things you want, one of them being money. The other two things could be as simple as having someone buy you a coffee or finding a free parking spot in a crowded lot. It's up to you.

Just be sure that whatever you write down is at least an 8 out of 10 rating in believability for you.

If you write down, "Someone is going to buy me an iPhone" or "I'm going to win $10 million dollars in the lottery" you probably won't believe it. If something is a 1/10 on the believability scale, then that's too much of a stretch. You're shooting yourself in the foot.

Pick something believable to you. You might say, "I want someone to buy me a Starbucks coffee," and that's going to be an 8 out of 10. Perfect. Go with that. That's step one.

Step #2: Visualize each item on your list daily.

Now take that list and start to visualise each item daily. What you want to do is visualize each item as if it's already been actualized.

However, don't get attached to the how and when. Let's go back to the coffee example. Don't worry about where the coffee comes from. Don't visualize a specific person buying the coffee for you. Just focus on the outcome. Coffee – what it smells like, how it tastes, how warm it is, what it feels like to hold it in your hands, and how great you feel that you've been able to create this for yourself.

Now let me give you a money example so that you understand the "feeling" that you are looking to evoke in this visualization. If you wanted to pay off all your debt in one swoop, what you would do is imagine that you got a ton of cash and paid off all your debt. Right now. It's completely gone.

Now this example might not be believable to you, but how does it make you feel? For most people, the word that comes to mind is relief. That's what I want you to feel – relief, it's done. It's complete. You want to feel relieved, as if it's already happened. *I've already paid the debt. I've already attracted the money.* You're going to feel relief. Do that for two to three minutes every day for each of the three things that you wrote down in Step 1.

That's the second step. Do this daily for the next seven days.

What's the next step?

Step #3: Acknowledge yourself as a POWERFUL creator.

Whatever shows up, shows up. And when it shows up, acknowledge yourself as a deliberate creator. Realize that you were the source of this creation.

One way to do that publicly is by posting your results in the comments at the original video I have posted on YouTube, you'll find the video to post your comments publicly. Plus, you'll see what others are creating, which might even inspire you to create something bigger.

You want to acknowledge yourself as a deliberate creator. This is important if you want bigger and better things to show up. When you acknowledge yourself, you're basically saying, "I intended to create something, and I've got this. Now I'm going to create some more cool stuff."

You've got to work within your current beliefs, and you've got to take baby steps. If you want bigger things to show up in your life over the next 12 months, two years, three years or even five years from now, start with this process and build.

7 DAY Manifestation Experiment

Step 1

**Write down a list of
3 things you desire.**

- Make one of them money
- Rate them on a scale of 1–10
- They must be believable
  to you

Step 2

**Visualize each item
on your list daily.**

- Picture the outcome
  (the end result)
- Feel the emotion as if
  it's already done
- Then, forget about it and
  go about your day as you
  normally would

Step 3

**Acknowledge yourself as
a POWERFUL creator.**

- When something shows up
  acknowledge the source (You)
- Realize that you are the Creator

Open Camera App on your Phone
to scan this QR Code and join the conversation.

I call this the 7-day manifestation experiment. I'm not asking you for a 30-day, 60-day or 90-day commitment. It's just seven days. Try it and see what happens. See what magic comes out of your life.

Here are some more results from ordinary people creating extraordinary results from the 7-day manifestation experiment:

"This is crazy! I just did the 7-day experiment yesterday. One of the things I asked for was $500.00. Well today, my husband, who is a contractor, was fixing a drain and pulled out a 14k gold bracelet and brought it home to me! It is 15 grams and has a scrap value of avg $300.00! I never thought this would come so quick!"

— Beth L.

> "I did this kind of thing before, many times. Last time I did it, I had been trying to find a tenant for my Mum's old house that was a money pit. Within 5 days I had a great new tenant! It really works! Living the dream!!!!!
>
> – Alison H.

Easy-peasy... 1-2-3

Now onto how to use intentions to shift your life.

Chapter 4

Using Intentions to Shift Your Life

> *"You may consider yourself an individual, but as a cell biologist, I can tell you that you are in truth a cooperative community of approximately fifty trillion single-celled citizens."*
>
> – Bruce H. Lipton,
> The Biology of Belief

It was a weekend in the summer of 2007 when I participated in T Harv. Eker's Millionaire Mind Intensive in Toronto. It was life changing. There must have been 1,000 people in attendance. I sold my Nissan 350Z to pay for the additional courses I purchased that weekend so I could continue to pursue my growth and potential.

During the course, we learned about affirmations. I started using the affirmations from the course. I was diligent and practiced these affirmations every day. I would say things to myself like, *I have a millionaire mind,* or *I am rich.* I was persistent and kept saying these affirmations every day for about 6 months.

I was determined. I believed in this. "I know this will work. I just need to keep doing it," I would say to myself. Yet nothing really changed in my life. That's when I realized it was because I wasn't accessing the subconscious mind. I wasn't internalizing the idea. I wasn't giving instructions to the 50 trillion cells in my body.

That's right! You have an estimated 50 trillion cells in your body. Every cell's got a respiratory, digestive, and excretory system. Virtually every cell's got an immune system. Cells have a nucleus - so they are "thinking" cells. Cells are like miniature people. Your brain is the government for the 50 trillion miniature people in your body. Every moment is a moment when you are having continuous communication with these citizens based on what you think and feel moment to moment.

Now the question is, how do you command the 50

trillion citizens of your body?

What do you tell them to do?

What do you say to them?

What commands do you give them?

Are you talking to them at all?

The answer is yes. If you get anxiety because you have an upcoming meeting that you are thinking about and you're feeling even a bit nervous about it, then that message gets sent to every cell (citizen) in your body. A nervous human creates nervous cells. Your cells respond to the way you think and feel moment to moment.

An intention is the instructions you give your 50 trillion cells. Your intent can be something positive or negative. It could be to heal something, attract something, create an opportunity, download new ideas, bring resources easily to you, attract people, whatever it is.

Take a moment to ask yourself, what intentions am I setting? What instructions am I giving to those 50 trillion cells right now?

The way to know the answer to that question is by how you feel. If you feel relaxed and peaceful, then you're telling your body to relax and be peaceful. If you're happy, then you'll have happy cells. It's up to you what commands you give your body.

When you set an intention, you're not setting a goal. A goal is something that you create outside of you. For example, reading books is something outside of you. Watching good content online is something outside of you. Using a vision board is something outside of you. All of these are part of your external reality. You may talk to yourself for short periods of time when you're reading a book, but the changes don't stick in your subconscious mind. The information is external.

An intention is an "inside job". It comes from within. That's how you create your reality. The only way an intention comes into fruition and becomes a reality is when the information and emotion you give those 50 trillion cells in your body has been accepted by the subconscious mind. You always want to set the intention by internalizing it first.

What most people are doing is simply setting goals, saying affirmations during the day, reading books, or watching videos on YouTube. There's nothing wrong with any of those things if you want to gain a deeper understanding of certain concepts. In fact, it's probably one of the reasons you're reading this book.

However, if you want to see a catalyst for real change in your life, then you'll need to give commands and directions to the 50 trillion cells in your body. You need to seed your subconscious with information and emotions. That way the intent is internalized and accepted as a fact.

> *"A cell is a 'programmable chip' whose behavior and genetic activity are primarily controlled by environmental signals, not genes."*
>
> – Bruce H. Lipton,
> The Biology of Belief

The Subconscious Mind

We all have a conscious mind and a subconscious mind. The conscious mind is the mind that you work with when you're awake during the day. It's the mind that you use to solve problems analytically. It's the logical mind. However, the conscious mind is somewhat limited in terms of its capacity to access and process information.

That's where the subconscious mind comes in. The subconscious is a database for everything. It stores your beliefs, your previous experiences, your memories, and your skills. If you have had bad (or good) patterns of behavior, those programs are in your subconscious mind. If you find it easy to stay healthy and fit, that's your subconscious programming

According to Emma Young in *New Scientist* magazine "Current scientific estimates are that some 95 percent of brain activity is unconscious." What that means is that your perceptions, your behaviours, and the state of your 50 trillion cells is controlled by your subconscious mind. This includes your habits and patterns, body function, creativity, emotions, personality, beliefs, and values are all primarily driven by the subconscious. If you want to see lasting change, then start with accessing the subconscious mind.

Think of your two minds, the conscious and subconscious mind, as an iceberg. The top of the iceberg is your conscious mind. It's just a tiny fraction of the total iceberg. The largest part of the iceberg, which controls its location, position, and buoyancy in the ocean waters, is mostly hidden by the water. That's your subconscious mind. It has the greatest power to control your destiny.

> *Your subconscious mind is like fertile soil which accepts any seed you plant within it. Your habitual thoughts and beliefs are the seeds which are being constantly sown within, and they produce in your life what is planted just as surely as corn kernels produce corn. You will reap what you sow. This is a law.*"

> – John Kehoe,
> Mind Power Into The 21st Century

The subconscious mind doesn't think or reason independently. It simply obeys the commands it receives from your conscious mind. If you focus on working with your subconscious mind for as little as 10 minutes a day, then you will unconsciously program yourself to focus on those aspects of your life during your day.

Think of your subconscious mind like the Matrix in the movie *The Matrix*. As soon as Neo enters the Matrix, he has access to all the answers and all the information he needs. Whatever he wants to create is available now. If he wants to learn Kung-Fu, he can do that instantly. If he wants to learn another skill or have another experience, again that experience is available instantly. Everything is available to Neo now.

You are Neo. You are the Creator. You can create whatever you want. Once you learn how to access those deep trance states in your subconscious mind and get past your analytical mind, all the answers are there. You can create whatever you wish. The most powerful tool you have as a human being is to create your experience. You have access to infinite wisdom. There is no limit to what you can do, be, or have.

If you struggle to stay fit, healthy, or attract the money you want it's because you have not accepted your desired end result as a present fact in your subconscious mind. If you had, it would be effortless. You would attract these experiences and many more without pushing yourself.

Your subconscious mind contains all information and all realities. Your job is to give those 50 trillion cells instructions to pull those ideas and realities into being using your subconscious mind.

What About Goals?

It's one thing to set a goal, but the real change happens when you internalize the idea. The intent must be internalized. It can't be something outside of you.

If you're in sales or in business and you have a lot of reluctance to conduct sales calls, then it tells me that you haven't internalized the intent. If the intent is internalized in the subconscious mind, then life gets easy. An external goal you wrote on a vision board or in your journal is not enough for it to show up in 3D physical reality because your subconscious mind has not accepted it as a present fact.

This is what I call a 'surface intention.' Surface intentions are not going to create a catalyst for change. So, the question now is, well what is?

It's setting a deep-level intention. It's when you get

beyond the analytical mind and plant an idea into your subconscious. The key is to understand the brain's natural cycles. We have four predominant brain wave frequencies:

- Beta, which is waking-day focus with external attention.
- Alpha, very relaxed daytime focus.
- Theta, deeply relaxed inward focus.
- Delta, sleep.

If you're going to set deep-level intentions, you must access the subconscious mind at the level of theta. That's the key state to creating lasting change. You can do that every evening when you go to sleep or every morning when you wake.

When you first wake up in the morning, you're in the theta brainwave state, and you're the most receptive to new information. It's when you're meditating, you're visualizing, you're doing this process first thing in the morning, and you feel as if the outcome has been realized. You're picturing your intent and you feel the emotions as if it's already complete. This must be done at the level of theta in order to get beyond the analytical mind.

So, how exactly do we set an intention?

You set an intention by picturing it and then creating emotions around it inside your body while you're in the theta brainwave state. This could be while you're day-dreaming during the day because you're already in a deep meditative state.

Or, as you're about to drift off to sleep, lying there not fully asleep, but not fully awake either, you start to visualize, you start to dream and think of the outcome as if it's already complete. That's what an intention is. It's giving instructions to the 50 trillion cells in your body so that you create a specific outcome. But that's just the first step.

The second step is you need to activate your intention by taking an action. What does that action look like? When you have that sales call, it means you ask the tough questions that take real courage. Or when you're looking to create a healthy body, you follow your intuition to reach out to a trainer or pay for a fit-ness service or buy healthy food. That's what action looks like.

Setting DEEP LEVEL Intentions

Part 2

Activate Your Intention:

- Follow your intuition and those inner 'nudges'
- When you feel inspired, act on that inspiration
- Action is effortless, and what you need to do next becomes obvious
- You're not forcing something to happen

Part 1

When You Wake First Thing in the Morning:

- Access the subconscious mind at the level of theta
- Key state to creating lasting change
- Feel as if the outcome has been realized and you can picture the outcome
- Key to giving instructions to the 50 trillion cells in your body

You see, anything you create on the inside will always come back to you as a download of new information to the inside. If you're just continually getting information from the outside you'll often get confused as to what to do, or what next step to take. You start to feel overwhelmed. But when you're setting deep level intentions and internalizing them, then your next move becomes obvious.

If you're taking the right action, you'll feel inspired. When you're inspired, choices become easy. They feel like the right thing to do. You start to feel like you're going downstream and no longer fighting against the current. That's how you know. You set the intention, and then you act from inspiration.

However, a lot of people skip this first step. They're reading all the right books, doing affirmations, and engaging in positive thinking, but they haven't created a catalyst for change. Those are all surface intentions. They are things outside of you. They're not deeply held in those 50 trillion cells.

If you give the correct marching orders in the correct way to those 50 trillion cells, they will execute for you every single time, without fail. That means when you get to step two, and you're acting on that intention, it just feels like the right thing to do. You don't question it. You're just going with the flow. And that is acting on the intent. That is activating the intention, so it materializes in your 3D reality.

The last step is to receive it. That can be as simple as opening an account or signing a contract. It's these fundamental things that will lead you to the end outcome that you want. Sometimes it means someone shows up in your life, but this time you are thinking differently about the information they have given you. You begin asking different questions. And those questions lead to new information and new actions.

So much of our programming, conditioning, and the way we think and perceive is based on our life experience when we were in that theta brainwave state from the ages of zero to six years old. Consequently, a lot of our careers are based on the people who were around us at that time.

Our role models, the people we looked up to when we were really small becomes our 'programming.' That programming gives us ideas and information that guides our future self image. The way we see ourselves is what we become. If you grew up in a family where almost everyone is an entrepreneur, then it is easier for you to see yourself as an entrepreneur. It becomes part of your 'inner being.'

If you want to change your programming, you've got to set deep level intentions and internalize them by daydreaming, meditating, and visualizing in those deep theta states. This isn't something you're going to learn in a day or immediately understand by reading a book. It's something you need to practice and experience. Through that experience you begin to understand how it works and you become motivated to keep doing it.

When you set your intention, you set it on the inside. You're setting that internal thermostat. You want to make X amount of money, set that intention on the inside. You want to have more joy in your life, set that intention on the inside. You want to have freedom, choices, and new experiences? Set those intentions on the inside. Picture it. Feel as if it's already done. Feel the joy, feel the love from that experience. You'll soon start feeling the abundance all around you.

If you're practicing this process during the day, or while you're out going for a walk, I guarantee you that it won't penetrate your subconscious. Your brain is normally in beta during the day, and so your attention is primarily focused on the external world. To get to a place where you are inwardly focused and where you can make real changes, you must get to theta. If this process doesn't penetrate your subconscious, then you just skipped the first step.

However, once you've got this dialed in, and you're starting to really align and make those changes internally where you can see it very clearly in your mind and you can feel it, then release it from your mind until your next meditation.

Now you can move onto step two throughout the day to act on that intention. You know you're acting on the intention when whatever comes to you, whatever feels downstream, whatever inspires you, you go for it, you run with it, you act on it.

Receiving can be as simple as signing an agreement and, boom, you're in the game. You need to set this appointment, someone sends you the money, then it's your job to deliver the service. That's receiving. It's an obvious action. It's when you are very clear about the next step. It's not pushing yourself to do something. You are feeling pulled toward doing it. That's just one way to use intentions to shift your life.

However, there are a lot of people who are not setting intentions. They're setting goals. They're reading affirmations. And they're not getting the results they seek. Maybe you have a goal to lose weight. You work hard, you put in the effort, but you find that the harder you work at your goal, the hungrier you get. And the hungrier you get, the more you eat and the more weight you gain. It becomes an endless cycle. The real catalyst for change happens when there is a shift internally that dramatically changes your beliefs, your perceptions, and your behaviours.

When you do get to step two, and you start to activate the intention, what you're doing is bringing more energy to the intention you've set. As you continue to act on it, you'll start to create more energy around your intention. Soon, it will materialize into the 3D world.

Think of it this way. Say you play with the idea that you're working with more clients or you're speaking in front of thousands or millions of people. Yet right now you're not speaking or selling to anyone. In fact, you don't even have any clients. However, if you keep setting your intentions internally and become emotionally involved with the idea, then you will eventually activate that intention by taking the action you need.

Guess what's going to happen next? Clients are going to show up, an audience is going to show up and people are going to want to work with you. That's how powerful you are!

An intention is something that you set every day because you are constantly creating. You have a bigger vision for yourself. You set your intention in the morning and then you go about your day, activating that intention and looking for opportunities to receive.

If you're doing this process repeatedly, setting the intention and then activating it, receiving gets easy. In fact, a lot of times you get something much better than what you originally set out for.

The easiest way to practice this process is to follow along with a guided meditation. I've put together a meditation for you to help you internalize your intentions. It's called the Magic Manifestation Meditation. You can download it here: www.magicmanifestation.ca You can also find each of the steps of the full meditation at the end of Chapter 9.

"Open Camera App on your Phone to scan this QR Code and download the meditation now."

Remember, an intention is simply the marching orders that you give the 50 trillion cells in your body. Once those orders have been accepted by the cells in your body, you will feel a sense of calmness. You will feel a sense of accomplishment. You will feel satisfied knowing that what you want is already on its way to you. You will stop worrying if or when something will show up in your life because you will have complete confidence that what you desire is on its way to you.

Now that we've shed a bit of light on how to set intentions, next we'll learn about what to do when manifesting doesn't work. We'll explore common pitfalls, how we get in the way of our own good fortune, and what to do about it.

Chapter #5

When Manifesting Doesn't Work

> *"If something you want is slow to come to you, it can be for only one reason: You are spending more time focused upon its absence than you are on its presence."*
>
> – Esther Hicks,
> The Law of Attraction

When I started my first coaching business, I didn't know how to make money. I panicked. I started to worry where the money would come from and that triggered more doubts in my mind. Because of that, I eventually went back to working as an engineer, but I learned something valuable from that experience.

When you're focused on a desire, or a dream you have, maybe you want to start a business-- whatever it is-- in the beginning, it can be exciting. A new relationship is exciting because you're focused on the fulfillment of it. You can feel that it's real, you feel the abundance of it, the truth of it.

The one thing that will prevent you from attracting what you want is focussing on the absence of it. When your brain comes in and you start to analyze what you want, you begin to focus on the absence of it. And when you're doing this, you're getting in your own way of your desires being fulfilled. It's important to remember that the Creator is supporting you in the fulfillment of your desire. Because of this, your desires have no timeline. They're always available.

The Creator is ready to serve up whatever it is that you want, at any time. However, what happens for many people is that when we focus on our desires, we start to analyze them. We get in our head about them. We start to feel overwhelmed by the things we used to be excited about. Suddenly, we're putting unconscious pressure on ourselves and the reason we do this is because we humans are conditioned to believe that we must work hard to get what we want. It can't be fun and easy. There must be something really hard I have to do!

This simply isn't true. I want to give you two techniques to help you stay in the flow so you're following the path of least resistance and you get what you want.

The first is to focus on the fulfillment of what you want. You can do that by meditating first thing in the morning to internalize your intent. Secondly, it's important to become aware of when you are instead focussing on the absence of what you want. You will know that's happening because you won't feel good. You'll start to worry and feel overwhelmed. These are all signs that you are focusing on the lack of what you want – not its fulfillment.

When that happens, move your focus to something else that gives you joy and makes you feel good, as opposed to the thing that you want. We put so much pressure on ourselves. We're like, "I've got to make this, I've got to create that, I've got to make this thing show up!" Unfortunately, what ends up happening is that for the first 30 minutes, it's amazing, and it feels good. But then suddenly, it starts to feel overwhelming. We start to experience anxiety and we put pressure on ourselves to create. Then, because of that, we're now focused on the absence of it. Well, guess what happens? You're getting in your own way. You're the one causing everything to stop or slow down.

Many times, in my business, I would create a business plan for the month. I would write down all the sales prospects I was speaking with and then rate each one based on how likely they are to close: cold, warm, or hot (ready to close in the next 30 days). Then I would put a value for each new client to close in the 'hot' category and do some math to figure out what my potential revenue would be for that month.

When I would create that plan, I could feel the fullness of my dream being realized. I could see the sales coming in month after month. I could visualize all the people I was going to help. I could feel the abundance. I would feel excited.

Two hours later I'd still be thinking about my business plan but instead I'd find myself focusing on the absence of my dream. Suddenly it would feel different. I'd feel that sense of anxiety and overwhelm.

This is what it looks like to get in the way of your dreams showing up for you. You start to change the frequency of your vibration. You go from 5Hz down to 2Hz just by thinking about it differently. When you do this, you attract very different physical results.

Inevitably, this is going to happen to you. So, when you begin to focus on the absence of your dreams, here's what I want you to do: I want you to build the habit of focusing on something else that gives you joy, that makes you feel good. Here's how to do that. First, always stay general.

What do I mean by that? Well, instead of focusing on earning a specific amount of money, paying off all your debt, and going on a cruise or traveling around the world, go more general. Just focus on what feeling all that will give you: freedom.

What does it feel like to be free? As you start to feel the freedom of it, you start to feel the guiding energy of the entire dream. Instead of focusing on the details, you start to lighten up. You start to feel less pressure. And guess what happens? That's when things start to unfold and fall right into your lap.

So again, start with meditation and feeling the fullness of what you want. It's best to do it in the morning when you first wake up because your brain is the most receptive and in a state of least resistance.

That's when you want to focus on your dream. That's when you want to focus on what you want. When you focus on your dream, if you're not clear exactly what it is-- the details of it-- just stay general. You don't need to focus on *how* it's going to show up. You don't need to worry about it *when* it's going to show up because when you do that, you're putting pressure on yourself. That takes you out of the flow.

Instead of thinking about the "how," just focus on asking yourself questions like *what would freedom feel like? What would it feel like to have choices? What would it feel like to feel joy?* Then just focus on those feelings in your morning meditation.

When you're finished your meditation, do your best to stay in that state throughout your day by focusing on things that give you joy and that make you feel good.

Let me give you a practical example. I have a client in the book publishing industry. We have been working together for about 10 months. We provide marketing for his business, and he has generated over 120 sales conversations from our marketing efforts.

However, he was only signing a small percentage of these conversations. *What is he doing on these sales calls,* I'd wonder? These are good leads! At least that's what I thought. So, I emailed him and said, "tell you what, let's get on a few sales calls together and I won't charge you anything upfront. I just want to help you sign these clients. If we sign some clients, just give me 10% of whatever we close."

He emailed me back saying he'd give me 20%!" Alright! Let's do this! I got on a few sales calls with him and quickly discovered that sales just aren't his strength. I also realize that for me these calls are a lot of fun. They're easy for me because I have a lot of experience running sales conversations. And now, there's more money coming into my business because I'm getting paid to close these sales calls for him.

All this to say that I was following my own advice:

- Focusing on the fulfillment of what I want.
- If I started to focus on the absence of it, I would

bring my awareness to something else that feels like fun.

After a few weeks of running these sales calls for this one client, I got the idea to run these sales calls for a few other clients as well. I figured why not? I have the time and it's fun for me. So, I emailed a few clients to let them know that this was a new service that I was providing for free, and that they could pay me a commission if and when we closed. A handful of clients signed up and we started taking calls. Life was getting a lot more fun!

Let me give you another example. The other day, I woke up, did my meditation, and felt great. An hour later, I started focusing on the absence of what I wanted. I started putting pressure on myself. I felt like I needed to know *how* it would show up, and I started to feel stressed. After an hour of this I thought, "I'm going to go to the gym. I need to do something with this energy."

So, I'm at the gym playing basketball. I'm feeling great. I'm having a good time.

About halfway through my workout, I get this text from a potential client. He says he's in. He wants to sign with us. I wasn't focusing on him becoming a client. I was doing something that gives me joy. I was playing basketball.

Throughout the rest of that day, I wasn't really focusing on my business at all. I wasn't' focusing on bringing in sales. I was just focusing on having a good time and having fun. Later, around 10:00 pm that evening, I checked my email and saw that I had received a deposit for $3,500USD. I'm thinking "where the heck did that come from?" It was from a guy I'd spoken with over 6 months earlier. He was now a client!

Again, I followed these two principles. I focussed on what I wanted in my morning meditation. I didn't know exactly what that was, but it didn't matter because I know I wanted freedom, I wanted abundance, and I wanted to have fun. Then I just focussed on the feeling and the *essence* of that. It's always safe to go general. You don't have to get too specific. You can just go general.

This is just my daily practice. When I realize that I

am focusing on the absence of what I want, I focus on something else that makes me feel good, gives me joy, and feels fun to me. I joke a little and try not to take myself too seriously. And guess what happens? I get ideas. I get inspired. Then I just follow that inspiration.

The Creator has no timeline. The Creator is always willing to give you what you want. You must get out of your own way. To do that, you need to become receptive. You allow it. You get into the fullness of your desires, of your dreams, or of whatever you want.

We all think we need to work hard to get what we want, and honestly - that is no fun. Why can't life be fun and easy? If you feel worthy of what you want, then it can be fun and easy.

When we start focusing too much on what we want, we start to focus on the absence of it. When you do that, it disconnects you from the energy that will give you what you want. This prevents you from attracting it.

So again, the key is that during your meditation, when you're in that place of zero resistance and not interfering with what the Creator has in store for you, that's when you focus on the fulfillment of what you want.

And then again, during the day, when you notice that you are focussing on the *lack* of what you want, consciously bring your awareness and thoughts to something else that gives you joy and makes you feel good. That's it!

You don't have to be super focused on exactly what you want and picture every detail. Start general and get into the space of focusing on freedom or having choices and options - the expansive feeling of abundance. Once you do that, you start to build momentum. You get a download of new information, or a new insight that changes you. You feel inspired, you act on it, and you follow through with it. Then you get another download. You feel inspired again, you act on it again, and you manifest the result. Trust yourself to wait for those moments, and the Creator will deliver - things will start to fall into your lap. Life starts getting good.

A few other caveats to help you stay in the flow of life and on the fulfillment of what you want:

Don't be too <u>attached</u> to someone specific.

For example, you want to marry someone specific, or you want 10 clients and have all the pictures of their faces. You can see them. Forget about that. Let it be a surprise. What I'm saying is don't be too attached to attract someone specific.

Instead, just focus on being in an intimate relationship and feel the excitement that goes with being in a new relationship, but don't get too specific as to who that person is. The Universe will always give you something better. The Universe knows. The Creator knows what you want. Just do your best to relax and have fun. This is a game.

Don't worry about <u>when</u> it's going to show up.

What happens many times is that we set an intention, we activate the intention, and then worry about whether it's going to materialize. We create a timeline for when it MUST show up. But this slows things down. We are now interfering with the creative process.

The Creator knows you must pay rent tomorrow. The Universe understands what signal and information you have sent with your intention. Trust that all is well, and all things will show up in divine time.

The answers always come. The more you practice this process, the more you will see this in your own experience. In fact, as you build momentum, you'll start to see more and more synchronicities show up in your life. If you start thinking about having more fun in your life, a friend may reach out to do something fun with you on the weekend. Maybe you're looking for more adventure in your life, and you've always wanted to travel across Europe. Just by focusing on that feeling and the spirit of adventure, you get an email or see a sign on the highway from a travel agency offering a discount on European vacations. Most times what you want doesn't show up the way that you expect anyways so be open to surprise.

Don't worry about <u>how</u> it's going to show up.

Give up the how. "How" has limitations built into

it. The more you focus on the how, the more you limit the possibilities. Focus on the bigger, more expansive picture of *how you want to feel* a year from now. That will take the pressure off and get you thinking bigger with less detail.

If you're going to focus on any detail at all, dig deeper into quantum physics and how the Universe works. Learn more about the human biofield and how it changes the radiant energy and the EMFs (Electromagnetic fields) around you. As you learn more about your gifts as a human being, you'll realize that you are in fact, the Creator of your world.

Continue to bring attention to your state of 'beingness' even as the results start to show up. Remember, it's this state of being that attracts your future results. Focus on what it feels like to have your object of manifestation fulfilled. Then relax. All is well.

Don't look for it.

When I say don't look for it, what I really mean is don't be on the lookout for evidence that what you want is on its way. Don't focus on how it will show up for you. Let it be a surprise. Trust in your ability to change your emotions (vibration) and your nervous system to tune in to what you want. Find a quiet place when you can focus on these questions to stay in the flow:

- What does it feel like to be free?
- What does freedom feel like?
- What would it feel like to have choices?
- What would it feel like to feel joy?
- What does it feel like when you're having fun?
- Where do you feel that in your body?

As you start focusing on the fulfillment of what you want, you'll start gaining momentum and you're going to feel better.

Limiting Beliefs

The following is a list of limiting beliefs that prevent you from attracting the abundance and joy that you desire. These are the preconceived ideas in your mind that are holding you back from intentionally creating your life. These beliefs don't serve you. They put a stranglehold on your ability to manifest the life you want.

Desire for Self-Punishment

Some of us have an unconscious desire for self-punishment. If you have an unconscious desire for self-punishment and you have a history of abusing alcohol, drugs, or being around people who don't serve you, or worse even, abuse you, life is going to be hard.

The key is to recognize that you don't want to live this way anymore and that you are enough. Be gentle with yourself and start making small changes to honor your boundaries and change your energy. It can be done. You can do this. Believe you are worthy of a better life, and it will show up for you.

Unconscious Debt to God

Some of us may feel we have an unconscious debt to God or the Creator. You don't believe you are worthy of abundance – you feel you must receive less, and God must receive more. You must be in servitude without getting what you deserve. You can't expect possibilities when you're living in limitation.

This old idea that you must provide penance and suffer here on this planet to benefit some 'greater God' is outdated. You originated from and are a piece of God. You are the Creator manifested in human form. You don't need to have less, while God gets more.

You literally have the technology in your body to create miracles. You are a wave of possibilities, and you are part of this benevolent energy of the Creator. You are a spark of God. Claim this. Know this. You are worthy of abundance.

Big Ego

Some of us struggle with our egos. If you feel that you are superior to all other beings, and are always caught up in your own ego, you will never create abundance. You've got to have humility. You are a partner with God. You must be 'ok' with the idea that there is a Creator that is taking care of things on your behalf – this partner in life is the one you can connect to at any time. Nourish that connection to the Creator and know that you are part of all things.

You must trust the idea that when you make a request from the Creator, there will be a response. In other words, you always have help manifesting your desires in physical form. You must understand that this benevolent loving energy only wants the best for you.

You can have the life that you want. You can change your life at any time. You can do that when you pray or meditate in the morning. When your mind is quiet, say these words quietly to yourself:

This belief is no longer serving me. I request to release it now. This feeling I have of being unworthy of abundance is no longer serving me. I request to release it now. These limitations have been interfering with my purpose and the work I am here to do on Earth at this time, and they no longer serve me. I request to release them now.

I am worthy of love. I am worthy of joy. I am worthy of abundance. Please release all limitations that prevent me from living my soul's purpose now. Thank you. I appreciate you. I love you.

You are a piece of God. Your entire being is an energetic wave of possibility. You can change at any time. You have free will. All that is required is your willingness to make peace with these limiting beliefs from the past and then focus on the fulfillment of what you want.

Next, you'll learn how to make sure your intentions are aligned with your own best interests and the best interests of those around you.

Chapter #6

Allow Things to Come to You

"Right now, in what I am about to say or do, do my desires stem from my lower or my higher self?"

– Wayne W. Dyer,
Wishes Fulfilled: Mastering
the Art of Manifesting

When I first raised my prices for my marketing agency, I lost more money than I made. Due to lack of experience, I had difficulty delivering the results I had promised to my clients. That created an internal conflict. A part of me really wanted the money and felt worthy of the money. I had visualized making a lot of money and felt good about it. But another part of me felt bad for the client because I didn't want them to lose money on our arrangement.

That taught me a valuable lesson in business and in life – that it's essential to always find a way that everyone will benefit from any transaction with you. That's the first key.

What I want you to do is ask yourself, if you were to get the things that you want, everything you meditate on and visualize - whatever it is that you want - more money, better relationships, spiritual awakening, ask yourself this one question: will it benefit everyone involved?

I guarantee that if you haven't got the things that you are looking to attract into your life, the answer to that question is No. Why would I say that? My belief is that God, Spirit, or the Creator – whatever name you use to describe this life force – is a benevolent energy that benefits all. The Creator does not take away something from someone to give to someone else.

That's an important distinction. Let's say you were to set an intention. You want to create something that benefits everyone involved. Let's also say that you're a salesperson. You know that if you sell more, you'll make more money.

Now think about the person getting your product or service in return for that money. Are they benefiting as well? Are all ships rising and gaining from this transfer of money? If the answer is no, and you're the only one benefiting, that's splitting the world in two. That's a duality where one person benefits and the other does not.

We human beings as a species are moving out of duality and into oneness. This means not only do I benefit because I made the sale, but the person also buying the product or service likewise benefits. We both elevate and gain because of this collaborative effort. That's the unity, the oneness that I'm talking about. If God or the Creator is one, then you can't split that life force in two.

Here's another example. Let's say you want a new job. You want a better paying job, a job that gives you more fulfillment. So, you ask yourself: will this benefit everyone involved if I take this job? If you can honestly answer yes to that question - that everyone involved will benefit and that you will feel more fulfilled - then you increase your chances of realizing that intention.

Maybe you've had jobs or you're looking for one right now, and you'd like to get paid more money. However, once you take the job and you start working for this new company, you feel miserable. Now, you're doing a disservice to yourself because not everyone involved benefits. Maybe the employer does, and you may earn more money, but you don't feel fulfilled. In that case, you're not benefiting from this intention.

Again, that's duality. That's a form of separation. If you are the Creator or a piece of God, then how could you be two? You can't. If something is whole, it cannot be split into two. You're back at this lower vibration, where there's duality. Remember, at higher vibrations, there's unity so everyone involved benefits. Everyone involved *must* benefit if you want to realize your intention.

Before you set an intention, always ask yourself: will this benefit everyone involved? If you get an absolute "Yes", then you'll find yourself surrounded by this benevolent energy of oneness that supports all things, that supports all life. Watch how quickly that will shift everything in your life.

You're never trying to take from someone so that another person has less. You must benefit everyone involved. Duality is a form of fragmentation. You can feel this in your body. This is where one part of you is, "Yeah, that would be a really good job," and then another part of you is, "but I won't be that happy," but you take the job anyway and then you don't feel fulfilled – you feel split in two.

Or you think, "Oh, I'd be really fulfilled if I took that job and I'd be happy," but another part insists, "I should be getting paid more because I'm worth it."

Duality is at a lower level of vibration. If you're evolving and growing (which you are if you're reading this book) then you're going to feel more comfortable taking the job that benefits all people involved. You're going to feel better because it will make you feel whole and complete. If you take the job because you just want to do the work that makes you happy, but you're not getting paid what you're worth, you'll feel incomplete, which is another form of separation.

You don't want separation. You want connectedness. You want wholeness. You want to support the whole of you because on some level you already know you are connected to all things, and all things are a part of you. Remember, everything is energy, and everything is connected.

Now here's something else to consider. This process of setting an intention that benefits everyone involved is a process of refinement. You must be patient as you're likely going to experience a bit of contrast. You may get a bit more of what you don't want in the beginning before you find what you do want. That's the process.

If, without a doubt, you can say that it benefits everyone involved when you're receiving more money, you're feeling more fulfilled, and the person buying that service from you also benefits, then you have a strong pure intention. That speeds everything up. Watch what happens next.

Once you have that pure intent, continue to do the deeds, and take the actions to make that intention a reality. Sometimes a small change in the way you approach it will make you more fully aligned with the vibration of this new field of intention. Just keep asking yourself that question, will this benefit everyone involved?

Once you know that everyone will benefit from being involved in this new intention, regardless of whether you intend to live on the beach, or you want more money - the way to know that you are on track is that it feels good to you.

Again, if you feel unfulfilled even though you're sleeping in every day and living by the beach without any financial concerns, but you don't feel a richness of spirit, then that's doing a disservice to you. Your soul is meant to feel full at all times!

You're not benefiting from this intention. It must be 100% aligned so that every ship rises - including yours.

Once you get that experience or feeling in a meditation, and you're like, wow, now everything feels like everyone involved benefits. There's no fear. There's no worry. There's no sense of feeling guilty for being the salesperson because you know that whatever the customer buys is going to benefit them more than what they paid for that product or service.

Once you get to this place where you know that everyone has benefited and are unified from the transformation of, for example, a sales transaction, then your job is just to focus on all those who benefited. Not only do you feel grateful, but you can feel *delighted* that the people you are serving are getting the very best of you.

When you get that new job and work with that new employer, they benefit from your service and contribution. You equally benefit from not only being happy and enjoying the work you do but also getting paid what you believe you're worth. That's when all ships rise, and when everyone involved is receiving the benefit. That's how you create intentions that allow things to come to you.

You might hear stories of people easily and effortlessly manifesting and attracting what they want, and wonder, "How the heck are they doing that?"

They are aligned in the sense that they've got a very

clear YES to the question: will everyone involved benefit? That's how you get into a state of allowing. It's not just about being grateful. It's about choosing intentions that benefit everyone involved. Here's another example of an ordinary person attracting money after practicing the 7 Day Manifestation Experiment:

"After listening to this (your video), I wrote down 3 things I wanted. One was to get $500, and one was for someone to pay for my car. Well, my boyfriend told me out of nowhere that he would pay for my car and I also received a check in the mail that I was not expecting! It works!! I was so happy I cried. Thank you for the video."

– Pisces G.

You Are More Powerful Than You Believe

The wiring of the way you think and perceive can be changed. This has always been a possibility for you. The key to change now is to understand the secrets of your brain from the day you entered this world until you were around seven years old.

During your infancy, your brain was young and developing and constantly in and out of the theta brain wave state. In this state, you were susceptible to the thoughts, perceptions, and views of the people around you, including your parents, teachers, and your role models.

As you'll recall from chapter 4, our brain has four predominant brain wave frequencies:

- Beta, which is waking day focus with external attention.
- Alpha, very relaxed daytime focus.
- Theta, deeply relaxed inward focus.
- Delta, sleep.

Theta is the key to changing your belief systems. Every day you wake up in the theta brainwave state automatically. It's the perfect time to start your meditation and begin to set your intentions because you have unrestricted access to your subconscious mind. It's when you're the most receptive to new ideas.

So that's the second key to creating your dreams. Use

this time of day wisely.

Here's the third key: the Illusion of Truth. The Illusion of Truth is a concept that states that your tendency to believe something is based on its repeated exposure and reinforcement. The more you repeat something, the more familiar it becomes. And the more familiar it becomes, the more believable it becomes.

Media companies use this concept in their marketing campaigns all the time. The repeated news and information you receive via mainstream or social media is used to change what you believe to be truth.

In fact, media companies have been using this psychological principle to change the thought patterns and beliefs of entire countries and mass populations for at least a century, if not longer.

But that is media companies. You are not a media company. You are an energetic possibility. You are a transmitting station of unlimited possibilities and have been given free choice to choose what information you believe and what you don't believe. You can use the Illusion of Truth to your benefit and change your beliefs. Once you do, your entire life changes. It all comes down to how we receive information and how often.

Many times, the more often we receive the same information or "new idea," the more familiar it becomes. The more familiar it becomes, the more believable it becomes, and at some point, we don't question that original idea at all. That's the Illusion of Truth in action.

Let me give you an example. When I first started my business online in 2008, I started selling eBooks for $25-$50. The first time I made $1000 in a single month, it was quite the transformation for me personally because a year before that I had no idea how I was going to make money.

I kept working my way up. A couple of years later, I created and started selling a $1,600 course. I was good at it. The sales came directly from a webinar, and I didn't have to do anything except respond to a few emails here and there to support clients who bought my product.

Fast forward a year or so after that, I decided to start selling a service for $5,000. To be honest, I thought it was going to be easy. I was wrong. I had a lot of negative things happen to me during this transition. Clients asked me for refunds on money I didn't have. Why? Because the service I was providing did not benefit everyone involved. I was still learning and didn't know how to get my clients the results they expected. It was a complete mess, but I learned a lot from that experience.

I learned that just because I sold a course for $1,600 doesn't mean I can go and sell a service for $5,000 and that it would be easy. It was hard for me because I didn't believe I could deliver for clients. I felt guilty taking their money. I had to learn how to deliver the service so that it was compelling and desirable for clients, but more importantly I had to believe that I could deliver. It had to benefit everyone involved.

This experience reminds of this quote from Dr. Bruce Lipton:

"Anything you work hard at. Anything you put a lot of effort into. Anything you sweat over to make it happen.

Why are you working so hard?

The answer is: Your programs and subconscious don't support that."

Since that time, I have had individual clients pay $25k - $48k for marketing services, and to be honest, it was easy. What I'm saying is that you may not see the results you want when you start in the beginning. There is a lot of resistance internally. You may not be choosing intentions that benefit everyone involved. You must have supportive beliefs to create and manifest your dreams.

Be patient and kind to yourself. Keep focusing on changing your internal state, your energy. Eventually, you will get to a point where you have the beliefs to support what you want, and then it will be easy for you.

There are two ways you can use the Illusion of Truth. The first way is to get information from the outside of you, like the ideas in this book, and internalize them so that you believe them. You may believe some of the ideas I have shared with you so far, but you may not believe all of them. And that's ok. You have free will to choose what you believe.

The second way is by getting information from the inside like new insights, downloads of information, or vivid dreams or visions you receive during a meditation or even in a deep sleep. These experiences help you receive information on the inside. Again, you have free will.

Now, you're probably not sitting there on a regular basis consciously thinking, "I want a million dollars". It's not something you have internalized or believe. If you don't have a million dollars, then that is the physical proof.

However, if you hear something often enough, or say a phrase to yourself with enough frequency, and you're in the right state when you do it, then you will start to believe it. That's how the illusion of truth works.

You are constantly creating your world. Here is one way that you can use the illusion of truth to create beliefs that empower you as opposed to ones that disempower you. As soon as you awake in the morning, your brain is naturally in the theta brainwave state. You feel groggy, sort of like you're tired, but you're consciously aware. You're in a very receptive state to rewire your beliefs, your perceptions, and even your habits.

If you start repeating something to yourself every morning, during that time of day, as opposed to just hitting your alarm and starting your normal routine, that's when the magic can happen.

Create Your Own Luck

Instead of going on "automatic" when you wake up in the morning, get in a chair or get into a meditation space, and constantly affirm something new like, *"I am lucky."* But keep saying it like a parrot. "I am lucky. I am lucky. I am lucky." Don't stop, don't stop, or think it's not working. You'll probably say, "Is it working?"

Forget all that. Go back to, "I'm lucky. I'm lucky." Keep at it. Wake up in the morning and again say, "I'm lucky. I'm lucky. I'm lucky. I'm lucky." As you do that for even a few minutes first thing in the morning, here's what's going to happen.

You're in the theta state, and you're going to start to feel lucky. It might only take a few minutes of this, or it might take a few days doing this every morning. But I promise that if you keep doing this, you're going to start feeling the luck.

Suddenly the words will change. In the beginning you started with, "I'm lucky. I'm lucky." Slowly you will start saying, "I feel lucky. I feel lucky." That's fine, it's close. Just keep going, "I'm lucky. I feel lucky. I'm lucky, I feel lucky."

Guess what happens? The more that you do that, the more familiar it becomes. The more familiar it becomes, the more believable it becomes to you. As you start your day after meditation, you will go out through your conscious day feeling and thinking that you're a lucky person. Now that's an empowering change!

You will start to feel luck drop into your lap. You'll notice something unusual will happen. At first it might just be a parking space that shows up unexpectedly, but then maybe your crush starts showing an interest in you, and voila...your "luck" is now starting to show up and you don't even have to do anything!

The Illusion of Truth is the tendency to believe information to be true after repeated exposure, regardless of whether the information is true or not in the beginning.

The fact is that you can train yourself to believe anything you want. It's your free will to choose, and you have the technology built into your human body to do it.

You have 50 trillion cells in your body, and you can instruct them, and tell them what you want them to do. Say to yourself, "I am lucky, I am lucky, I am lucky," and those cells will respond to the governor of your body: your brain. Those cells will follow your instructions, but you've got to be in the right state in the morning when you first wake up for that first five minutes. Then just keep doing it for days until it feels true to you.

Remember, the more you repeat something to yourself, the more familiar it becomes. The more familiar it becomes, the more believable it becomes to you.

Instead of having someone else programming and filling your mind with beliefs that don't serve or empower you, why don't you do it yourself?

It's your choice. Choose wisely.

Here's another story from Renu about attracting money and miracles using the 7 Day Manifestation Experiment:

"Omg, I must say - it works. I asked for $1500 and received $2500 within 3 days. I asked for a few clients to sign up with me I have signed up 2 clients already in 5 days. I asked for my son's admission in KG in one of the best schools, and I am getting options & in the process of finalizing.

I acknowledge LOA is powerful. I am so so grateful. Thank you so much for this Info. God bless all & your wishes come true!!"

– Renu D.

The benevolent energy of the Creator doesn't take away from someone to give you what you want. This energy benefits everyone involved. When you set your intention to get what you want, remember that all ships must rise. You can create your own luck.

Next, I'm going to show you how your body has been intentionally designed to create miracles. I'm going to give you examples of how our biology sends and receives information like a broadcast station, and how you can align your energy to connect to this information and insight so that you manifest your dreams.

Chapter 7

Acknowledge Yourself as the Creator

"If you have the ability to imagine it, or even to think about it, this Universe has the ability and the resources to deliver it fully unto you, for this Universe is like a well-stocked kitchen with every ingredient imaginable at your disposal."

– Ester Hicks, Ask and It Is Given

I recently got together with some old friends at a cottage in Northern Ontario, Canada. We had a great time, but what I find really fascinating is how this weekend with friends came together. Two months prior, I had been talking with these few friends about getting together, but we had no idea where we should gather.

At the same time, my wife and I were looking for a place to live in Canada as we finished our eleven-month tour in the US. We had been travelling but we wanted to find a place to settle in Canada. When my wife was looking for places to live, she came across the immaculate three-bedroom waterfront cottage.

I remember looking at the photos online and saying to myself, *this place is perfect.* So, I booked it. Now the thing with Northern Ontario is that the weather is always a gamble. You can have rain one day, and a hot sunny day the next. You never know what you're going to get.

When I saw those online photos, all I could think was, "this is perfect!" I had this overwhelming feeling that the cottage would be perfect on that specific weekend. Now here's what fascinates me. We had rain for about two weeks, but as the weekend with my friends approached, the rain and cool temperatures lifted, and Mr. Sun was back! We couldn't have asked for better weather. It was hot and we were on the lake all weekend.

The day after my friends left, the clouds came back, and it started to rain. Was it a coincidence or was the feeling I'd had been some form of telepathy? Was I being provided with information about the future through the field of intention?

I'll let you be the judge of that. But what I can tell you is that the human body is designed to be more receptive to subtle vibrations and information not available at the conscious level. That's what we'll talk about next.

Your Brain and Nervous System

You have a brain that allows you to "fire and wire" new synaptic connections every time you think a new thought. New thoughts create new connections, and these new connections create new circuits to allow electrical signals to travel and activate new chemicals (emotions) in your body.

With repetition and regular practice, you can train your nervous system to feel the emotions you want to feel. You can train yourself to perceive what you want to perceive. You can create new thoughts. These thoughts color your perceptions to shift your vibration and your reality.

Pineal Gland

In the middle of your brain, you have something called the pineal gland that contains tiny crystals. These crystals are piezoelectric sensors, which can convert mechanical pressure into EMFs (Electromagnetic fields). Think of your pineal gland as a broadcasting tower for new frequencies and new information.

Pineal gland crystals are activated through deep meditation and deep breathing. During deep breathing exercises, the fluid in your spine circulates from the base of your spine up through cavities in the skull, just like a pump moves water.

Your breath acts as the 'pump' to move this spinal fluid. As the pressure and force from the spinal fluid builds in the pineal gland, it activates EMFs so that you can send (broadcast) or receive information like a satellite. Your pineal gland is the satellite that connects you to the field of intention.

"The act of inhaling and bringing that breath all of the way to your brain with passion, and squeezing those [internal] muscles, you're exerting pressure against that pineal gland. As you start to pressurize those stacked crystals [in the pineal gland] you begin to produce a piezo electric effect. Now you're taking a mechanical stress and turning it into an electrical charge. All of a sudden when they become electrically activated, the pineal gland is becoming like a radio antenna, and now it can pick up frequencies faster than the speed of light.

— Dr. Joe Dispenza

In Chapter #2, we discussed Harold Saxton Burr's work to measure bio fields and his theory that these fields were creating our biology; that if you change the field then you change matter. The planet, and all matter in the Universe is also created from a field, and we can refer to that field as 'the field of intention.'

When you send information you are using intent, and when you receive information, you are using your intuition. All of this is standard equipment in the human body. You can send signals (intent) and receive signals (intuition) from the field.

The Human Heart

The heart is not just a pump for the blood in your body. It's the most powerful electromagnet in the human body. When you are in a super coherent state, the electromagnetic field created by the heart can be measured up to 10 feet outside of the body. That means vibrations and fields of energy can be measured and that you are influencing physical matter outside of your body. That's how powerful you are!

Let's say you're at a live concert and there are 10,000 people in the stadium. If 100 out of every 10,000 people in that venue are clapping their hands in synchronicity, then that's incoherence. However, if all 10,000 people in the stadium are clapping in sync together, then the sound in that venue gets amplified and there is way more energy. Super coherence is when all 10,000 people in that same audience are clapping totally in sync – that's a lot of energy! And that is what it will feel like in your body when you are in a super coherent state.

Remember the yogurt example from the documentary *I Am* in chapter #2? That's how powerful your heart and emotions are. The way you feel is important because it's constantly creating a field that affects matter locally and non-locally.

Not only does the heart affect matter, it's also a great receiver of new information. When you get new ideas or inspiration, that is the heart sending information to your brain to be processed so that you feel inspired and take action. Yes, the heart really does all of that. The way you feel matters. It's the same when you're angry or upset, except then it creates incoherency.

When you're upset, then you're incoherent and that means you have less energy and less cooperation from the cells (citizens) of your body. In this state there is more disorder, you feel that you have less energy, and you feel disconnected. You don't feel like yourself.

The way you feel matters. When you're super coherent, you feel whole and complete. You feel as if you are one with all things. You feel connected. You feel that you are in the flow and that life is perfect. You feel that nothing can go wrong. That is when all the cells in your body are in order.

Pay attention to how you feel. Mediation is a good place to start. It helps you become aware and channel your energies to create positive emotions and the magnetic field of the heart so that you feel super coherent.

You can practice my free Magic Manifestation Meditation here: www.magicmanifestation.ca

"Open Camera App on your Phone to scan this QR Code and download the meditation now."

Energy Centers

You have eight energy centers in your body and one of them is the heart. All these energy centers are "thinking brains" that affect your energy, mood, and perceptions. The bottom three energy centers (root chakra, sacral plexus, and solar plexus chakras) store past traumas, activate stress hormones, and keep you in a state of reaction and panic when they are out of balance.

With regular meditation, deep breathing, and other techniques you can re-balance these energy centers so that you remain in a state of coherence, so that you are aligned with your intent. Being coherent allows you to easily have more energy, vitality, clarity, and confidence. You become more trusting of yourself and feel more at peace.

The point is that there is nothing wrong with you. In many cases, what we label as 'wrong' is actually rooted in trapped energy in these lower energy centers. You are a divine being and sometimes a simple re-balancing of your energy and auric field is all that is needed to get you back to a place of peace and joy. Change the energy and you change your life.

You are the Creator. You are a piece of God. God is a piece of you – you are one with God. There is no separation. You are the co-Creator, and you have the power to create what you want. In fact, you are designed to perform miracles. You are a stream of consciousness that is continually manifesting and creating your world. The key to taking control and living an absolute blissful life is to use the technology you have been equipped with at birth.

Open the Satellite Wi-Fi Connection to Your Soul

There are two things you can do that will help you connect to the satellite Wi-Fi connection to your soul. One is to practice having an open heart (super coherence) and the other is to have a clear pineal gland.

Remember, the pineal gland has tiny crystals that convert mechanical pressure into Electromagnetic fields. These fields are activated by deep breathing. When you're breathing these deep breaths, your lungs are opening and closing, the spinal fluid goes up your spine into a cavity in your brain, and then it comes back down. It's just a circular loop.

Normally the spinal fluid takes about a day to circulate from the base of your spine all the way up to your brain and back again. But when you're practicing a technique like deep breathing, the pace accelerates and the fluid speeds up. As the velocity of the fluid increases so does the pressure of that fluid. Once the pressure is applied to the piezoelectric sensor (pineal gland) in your brain, it converts that mechanical pressure into EMF and electrical signals that broadcast your desire to the field.

When you're in that deep meditative state, your only job is to provide the information and the emotion for whatever you want to create. That's it.

If you want to become more connected to Universal Intelligence, or the satellite Wi-Fi connection to your soul, you need to be able to send and receive new signals and new information. Sending signals is done by setting your intention in your deep meditative state. Receiving information is done with an open heart.

As you surrender to your intention during the day

without forcing it into existence, with practice, you'll naturally get amazing visuals and 'downloads' from the field. This information can come to you as mystical experiences, new insights, or a new way of thinking about your dreams.

How to Ask & Get What You Want from the Universe

What follows is an exercise you can use to attract more of what you want, and less of what you don't want. The basic premise is that you're an energetic possibility and you have a heart, a pineal gland, and a nervous system you can utilize to change your frequency of vibration. When your vibration changes so does your reality. What you're doing is using the tools in your body to align with the energy of the new possibility.

#1: Make a List that Delights You

Number one is to make a list - a list of things that delight you. Be sure to do this first thing in the morning when you wake. First you must realize that you don't have what you want (yet) because you haven't made the necessary vibrational changes. By putting your focus on what delights you, you begin to feel satisfied. As you continue to feel satisfied, you will draw into you more things to be satisfied about.

As you're making your list and thinking about those things that 'delight' you, you're going to start to feel more satisfied with where you are in your life. That's the first phase.

So, start by making your list and writing down a few experiences that delight you. Then check in with yourself. How does it feel? Let's say you write down something like, "I'm delighted that I have a dog." Close your eyes and check in with yourself. How do you feel about what you wrote down?

If you say, "Yes, I love my dog. She makes me so happy." Then keep going through your list and continue to write down 10-20 more things that delight you. Keep asking yourself the question: What am I delighted about?

As you contemplate this question, you will get more and more ideas surfacing that delight you. This might take just 15 minutes to complete, or it might take an hour. It depends on how you have trained yourself to think.

If you are in the habit of constantly beating yourself up for not getting what you want, then it could even take a few hours to start to feel that glimmer of satisfaction. That's okay. That's the work. That's the effort required. As you continue to move in this direction, the feeling of satisfaction will 'well up' in your body, and then you're ready to move to the next phase.

#2: Think About Your Outcome

Now that you've got that feeling of satisfaction in your body, you're going to start thinking about your outcome. But you're not going to think about it the old way – that wasn't working. You're going to start thinking about what you want and feel satisfied that you have it or that you are in the process of having it.

Remember, you don't have what you want yet. We're trying to get you in a different state so that you feel the new possibility, and so that you feel the frequency of the new timeline. Start by making your list of delight. Then think about the *outcome* you want and feel the satisfaction of it. Feel delighted it is on its way to you.

Contemplate what it would feel like if you already had what you wanted. Then you're going to begin to think about the outcome and feel grateful for that outcome. Feel the satisfaction that it is coming to you.

Now just be patient with yourself. You can do this. Make your list and think about your outcome as if you already have it now. Practice feeling delight for the outcome, even though you don't have it yet. The more that you do this, the easier it becomes.

#3: Stay General

The third phase can take you anywhere from 20 to 30 minutes. Or it could take you an hour or more. It depends on what state you're in. If you're in a negative state, it might take you more time.

The third phase is to stay general. What do I mean by that? When you're thinking about what you want, you want to pick something and stay more general.

Here's what not to do:

If you want to keep the relationship you have with your partner, or you want this specific job, stay more general by asking, what would that feel like to be in the comfort of a loving relationship or companion? What would it feel like if I had that *type* of job? What would it feel like to have job security? Don't be too attached to someone or something specific.

Before my wife and I went down to Florida to live for seven months, because I love the beach, I would visualize the beach and that was it. Nothing more, just the beach. We got a spot just 10 miles from the beach. Everything worked out. It was very smooth and in the flow. That was because I stayed general. I wasn't too attached to where we were going to be in Florida.

So again, think about your outcome as if it has already happened. Feel the satisfaction of it but stay general with it. The reason you want to do that is if you get too focused on one thing, you start to get attached. Once you get attached, then you're expecting and wanting it. And that's the problem. If you want it, or you're in a state of 'wanting,' it means you don't have it.

You want to be in the state of feeling as if you already have it, knowing it's coming, and you are feeling grateful that it's already here. Remember, if you're wanting it, it means you don't already have it and that you're in a totally different vibration.

Stay general and be open to the feeling of whatever that general experience gives you. When you start to see things show up - even when your dream starts to materialize - don't change the way you think about the outcome too much.

You can add details to it, but don't get too attached to any specific possibility. Going back to my Florida example, I stayed general. Even after I knew where we were going, I'd go back and visualize the beach.

Sure, I'd look at photos online before we left for our trip - but I would stay general. And like I said, we ended up living near the beach. Stay general, even after you know what it is that is going to materialize. If you do that, it's going to make it easier for you to ask for something from the Universe.

Here's another story of someone using the 7 Day Manifestation Experiment to attract a brand new car:

> "This really works. Ok, so my car broke down and I couldn't get a loan for a car ANYWHERE. I did what Steve said and BOOM, I was able to purchase a car today! I do have payments on it but still I asked for a new car and I got it..!!!"
>
> – Sharrice B.

Your body has the most advanced technology on the planet. You are a broadcasting station that sends and receives information from the field of intention. As you deliberately direct your focus, you begin to get answers and insight to help you on your journey so that you manifest your dreams into physical reality.

That's the new human, and that's where we are going on this planet. As you begin to grasp an understanding of how powerful you really are, many more possibilities will open in your life. As you explore these possibilities, you're going to gain a new perspective of who you really are, and that's the new human.

Chapter #8

the New Human

> *"Meditating is also a means for you to move beyond your analytical mind so that you can access your subconscious mind. That's crucial, since the subconscious is where all your bad habits and behaviors that you want to change reside."*
>
> – Dr. Joe Dispenza,
> Breaking the Habit
> of Being Yourself

Many years ago, I had an episode of vertigo while working as an engineer. Vertigo is basically a condition where you get these terrible dizzy spells. It's an imbalance in your nervous system. You can't eat. You can't drive. You can't do very much if anything at all.

During this one episode of vertigo, I went to drive somewhere and almost crashed my car. I had to go back to the house, park the car in the garage and lay down on my bed. When I walked inside the house, I ended up vomiting from too much movement.

I couldn't do much of anything for an entire month. I even had to take time off work. Vertigo can be severe, but it's not commonly understood why people get it and how to treat it. I've had dozens of these 'dizzy spells' for my entire life from my mid 20s until just a few years ago.

The last time I had vertigo was Christmas 2019. I had been eating quite a bit of gluten and eggs, which is normal for me at that time of year because I love pastries and cookies. When I eat eggs or gluten, I often get a stuffy nose or congestion. This can happen within hours of eating but sometimes it shows up the next day. In some cases, these mild symptoms can lead to full blown vertigo.

On the Thursday after Christmas, I decided to go for a three-mile run. It was the holidays, and I hadn't been eating the best, so I decided to take it easy. I'm not going to push myself; I'd thought to myself. Just a nice run to get some fresh air and some exercise.

The following day was Friday. I woke up congested, so I took the day off to rest. When I woke up on Saturday morning, I had full blown vertigo. I started to panic.

I could feel the imbalance right away. It was like a 9 out of 10, 10 being the worst I've ever had. I felt like I'd drank an entire case of beer, even though I hadn't had any alcohol for at least a week. I laid back down. I was pretty upset with myself because this had happened before from indulging in baked goods. I couldn't drive. I could barely walk. Eating was out of the question. I could barely drink water.

What's the first thing I do?

I went to my old human. I had anxiety. I was upset. I was frustrated at myself more than anything because I was thinking "why am I getting sick?" I wanted to be healthy. I wanted to be energetic. I wanted to be full of life.

I went to my wife, who's a wealth of information on alternative health. She recommended that I start drinking celery juice. Her rationale was that these pathogens feed off gluten and eggs. Eliminate the 'food source' for these pathogens, and you eliminate the pathogens. As the viruses died, my health and well-being would return back to normal.

There's not a lot of science to backup her claim, but I trust her and the tens of thousands of people who have healed their illness using this process. I was all in. We started with two glasses of celery juice that morning. I could barely get it down. I was totally out of balance. It was intense, but I drank the juice, and I went from a nine out of 10 dizziness to an eight out of 10. There was a bit of improvement, but not much. I was frustrated.

Later that afternoon and that evening, the New Human kicked in. I saw some of my old self-help books on a bookshelf and I reminded myself that I'd been here before. I had been sick and feeling miserable before. I remember feeling frustrated, but also that I could heal my body at any time. I remembered who I am. I remembered that I have the power to heal my body at any time I choose. I have free will. I can think and create whatever I want. I can heal instantly if that's my wish.

You see, I forgot who I was. I forgot that all I had to

do was go inside and generate a new state of be-ing. That I have the power to do this. We all do. It's standard equipment for the new human.

So that night as I was lying in bed with everything spinning around me, I started to imagine. I started to dream. I started to feel as if I was healed. Now physically, I still felt this imbalance. But I was focusing as much as I could on the new image, the new state of be-ing. I imagined that I was running. I felt like I was play-ing hockey and doing the things that I love to do. I felt healthy and fit. I focussed my intent on that image and what it feels like to be that person.

Again, the next morning, I still had vertigo. I wasn't' healed, but I did my meditation anyway. I got into that deep trance where I am beyond the analytical mind and just feeling my body totally healed. I must have been in that meditation for at least an hour. I got up from my meditation still in that deep trance and feeling good. I had this energy and this knowing that I was totally healed. I expected to heal because I could see myself healed. I finished my meditation with this knowing that 'all was well.'

When I finished my meditation, I went through the protocol. My wife made me 32 ounces of celery juice. I drank the juice. The vertigo was still there at about an 8 out of 10. I was still dizzy as hell. It was intense, but I knew I was going to heal, and I drank the juice. It took me almost an hour to drink that celery juice, but then something miraculous happened.

Within an hour, the dizziness started to subside. I started to feel like myself again. One hour after drinking that celery juice, the intensity of the vertigo fell from an 8 out of 10, to a 2 out of 10. The process had worked! I was starting to feel normal again. All I could say was, "wow" and I started to cry.

Two days later, I went for another run, and I was totally fine. I haven't had vertigo since. I now know exactly what I need to do. I can heal myself and you can too. You are that powerful. That's the new human. That's what is possible for you. That's what is possible for all of humanity.

We can heal quickly. You have the tools to do it.

"I know that you have chosen to come to this place, and to get here [Earth]. It's like entering the Olympics. It's like getting on the Olympic team. You have made it to the opportunity to this dimension that we call the human experience."

– Dannion Brinkley,
Beyond Belief with George Noory:
Lighting Strikes

Becoming the New Human

The new human is much different and much smarter than the old way of being or the old human. The new human is a creative creature. The new human uses advanced technology built into the human body to create. If you're reading this book, you're on your way to becoming a new human. You're getting these upgrades as part of the ascension process. It's an exciting time to be alive.

One of the big differences between the old human and what I'm calling the 'new human' is the way we solve our problems. Problems are not going away, but the way we solve them is going to change in a dramatic way.

I used to get anxious when I had a problem in the past. It could have been a health issue, a relationship issue, or it could have been a money issue. I would get anxiety because I was focusing on the problem.

That anxiety would translate into very intense action. For example, if I was looking for a solution to market something online because my business wasn't doing as well as I would have liked, I would become very focused searching for answers. I would read article after article online. As a result, I was downloading a lot of information through my conscious mind.

Sometimes I'd lock myself in my office for hours while doing these searches. As I was going through the motions, I would feel tired, so I'd grab a coffee. That would get my adrenaline going again. That adrenaline would kick my brain back into high 'beta' and activate my analytical mind.

That's the old human. Now, I'm not saying there isn't any value in getting information from the outside. There is value in the process. However, I can tell you that the new human is so much wiser. It's so much more intelligent. The new human is going inward. The new human is tuned in to the connection to the divine. As the new human, you have an understanding and realization that everything is connected on a fundamental level.

As soon as you connect by going into those deep trance states in your meditation, your brain goes into theta, and that's where you find all the answers. You let the answers come to you through meditation as you get a vision, hear a tiny whisper, or gain a new insight. You're not looking outward for answers. You're going inward. Your intuition grabs your attention and guides you in a new direction. That's one element of the new human. The answers are coming from the inside.

Now each of us is at a different place in this transition. Some of us will be afraid of making these changes. Some of us will embrace them. Some of us have already started using these gifts and are shocked and confused that others haven't. At the end of the day, you have free will to choose what you will and won't do.

When it comes to manifesting, the new human has a higher degree of trust. You trust your biology. You trust the technology in your body to make changes to your nervous system and your emotions. Those emotions change your vibration, and that leads to new changes in your circumstances and your environment. You allow your subconscious mind to guide you. When you do this, the answers become obvious. That's the new human. That's the smart human.

These changes are not going to happen overnight. In the beginning, you may notice that you're more sensitive to certain people. Your level of discernment for the truth has been refined. You know when someone is lying to you or intends to lie to you. You have an ability to 'pick up' on the vibrations of other people and information that is unseen. This informs you whether those around you are well meaning souls or not.

That's the smart human, and that's where we're going. If you are reading this book, you already have this sense. You may be in the early stages, but you have it to some degree. These changes are starting to amplify and accelerate, even for those who are new to this process.

The smart human is about creating a new vision, feeling as if it's already done, and trusting what shows up. It's about having more fun. The new human knows that how they feel matters. How you feel is how you vibrate as a possibility. Change your vibration and you change what's possible.

As the new human, you have unlimited access to the benevolent energy of the Creator. That means you need to be prepared and ready to receive BIG TIME. If you are getting a nudge from the Creator to start exploring natural talents or a new career opportunity, be open to these nudges from within.

Now is the time for finding new ways to use your unique abilities and improve your life. You can literally live from the level of intention to create your life. Once you believe in this idea at a cellular level, your ability to manifest and create will be amplified. Don't waste this opportunity to access your true self and your true gifts. Honor who you are.

Magic Manifestation Meditation

If you'd like to start meditating, I've created one for you. Here's a walk-through of the meditation so that you can read along before you try it yourself:

I want you to close your eyes and take a deep breath with me. Once you exhale, uncross your legs and un-cross your arms. Now what I want you to do, is im-agine a location in time and space, that's about 20 feet to the left of you keeping your eyes closed.

I want you to imagine some location in space and time, that's about 20 feet to the left of you. I want you to imagine in your mind's eye, that location, it might be inside your home, it might be outside your home.

In a moment, what I want you to do is I want you to pull the energy from that location with the breath and then exhale through the top of your head.

Let's do that together.

Deep inhale. And exhale.

Deep inhale. And exhale.

Deep inhale and exhale.

Now what I want you to do is I want you to imagine a location in time and space, keeping your eyes closed, that's about 20 feet in front of you.

Again, find the location in time or space, that's about 20 feet in front of you in your mind's eye as best as you can. Visualize it and see it.

Once you have that location or some sort of landmark to represent that location, I want you to take a deep breath in, let's do that now.

Inhale. And exhale,

Inhale and exhale.

Deep inhale, and exhale.

So far, you're doing great. Now what I want you to do is I want you to find a location in time and space that's 20 feet to the right of you. And I want you to find a landmark that represents that location.

And again, in a moment, I want you to think that every time we breathe in, you're pulling the energy from that location into the lungs as best you can. You're pulling that into your body, filling the lungs, expanding them like a balloon and then exhaling through the top of your head. Okay, let's do that together now.

Again, deep inhale. And exhale.

Inhale and exhale.

Then inhale and exhale.

Now this time, what I want you to do is I want you to focus on a location that's 20 feet behind you in time and space, and find a landmark that represents that location, as best you can.

This time, what I also want you to do is I want you to focus on that location that's 20 feet behind you as best you can. And I want you to imagine that there's this delightful, pleasant energy in that location. You might even think of someone you love or something that you love in that location and just imagine it in that location 20 feet behind you.

Now what I want you to do (in a moment), is we're going to use the breath to pull that loving delightful energy to fill the lungs, expand them as best you can, and then exhale through the top of your head. Remember, each time we breathe in, we're pulling in that delightful, pleasant energy and then exhaling through the top of the head. Let's do that now.

Deep inhale. And exhale.

Then inhale and exhale.

Deep inhale and exhale.

Again, just moving that energy from those locations, and each time you breathe in, you feel it more inside your lungs - inside of your chest, that delightful loving energy, and then you exhale through the top of the head.

And each time you breathe in and out, you feel more

energy, more delight, more intent, and more of that loving energy. Now I want you to go back to the left. I want you to focus on a location that's 20 feet to the left of you, in your mind's eye. But this time, I want you to imagine some delightful magic manifestation energy in that location. Whatever you imagine, that would be that delightful, pleasant energy of your goal being complete and your dream realized.

Just feel that delight, just feeling so delighted that not only you're benefiting from this dream, but that all the other people that are in your life, they're benefiting as well.

If you provide a service to people in business, you want to see that delight in your clients, in your customers, in your followers, and just being so delighted that they're getting so much from what you're providing that delight, that's what you're looking for. That's the feeling.

You want to focus on that delightful energy, as best you can, in that location, 20 feet to the left of you.

And then what we're going to do in a moment is we're going to use the breath to pull that energy into the lungs, expand the lungs, and then exhale through the top of the head. So let's do that now.

Deep inhale. And exhale.

Deep inhale. And exhale,

Then inhale and exhale.

Awesome, you're doing great. Now, what I want you to do is focus on a location that's about 20 feet, in time and space in front of you. And again, just bringing that delightful, manifestation magic – that feeling of delight and whatever you're doing to serve the world, how it's serving other people, that delight, that's what we're looking for: that feeling of feeling delighted that something you did is serving someone else. And they're feeling in a state of joy because of what you did for them. And then allowing that joy to come back to you in any form, or any material way that works best for you.

Again, just focus on that location, about 20 feet in front of you, as best you can, focusing on that delightful, pleasant energy of your service or what you do - your contribution serving others, and how delighted you feel that others are receiving your service and that you are being of service. Keep focusing on that delight, that delightful energy, that pleasant, joyful energy in that location about 20 feet in front of you. And then in a moment we're going to pull that energy into the lungs, expand them like a balloon as best you can and then exhale through the top of your head. Let's do that now.

Inhale and exhale.

Again, inhale and exhale.

And inhale. And exhale.

And inhale. And exhale.

Each time you breathe in that energy, filling your heart with more and more of that pleasant energy. That delight.

What I want you to do now is we're going to do a few breaths together. I want you to let go of your dream. I want you to let go of that energy and just let it sit. You're not trying to control it or fix it. And we're going to take a few breaths together right now. Just to let it go.

So deep inhale and exhale.

Deep inhale and exhale.

Again, deep inhale.

And just let it go, exhale.

Now just go back to noticing and watching the body. Maybe thoughts you're having, it might be feelings you're having. Don't attach to any of the thoughts or feelings. Just watch them and notice them as best you can.

You're not trying to change anything or fix anything, you're not trying to control anything, you're just noticing and watching as best you can. Take another deep, deliberate breath with me deep inhale. And exhale.

Again, just noticing and watching the body, you might notice there's some tension in the body or some heaviness, that's okay, you're not trying to get rid of it or control it, just notice it. And just watch it as best you can.

Now, when you're ready, what I want you to do is open your eyes.

You can bring manifestation magic into your heart once a day. That's how you become a channel for the Creator. That's how you align with the field of intention. You go deep into your subconscious through meditation. Do that, and you'll gain the information that is going to draw you closer to your dream or goal.

You can download the full guided meditation and follow along for free at: www.magicmanifestation.ca

Your life experience and the reality you create for yourself is a result of where you focus. If you focus on the fulfillment of what you want, then life is grand, it's easy and it's a lot of fun. If you focus on the lack of what you want, then life gets hard, and you wonder why. You start to have doubts and you start to question yourself. If you want to see where your focus is, then just look at your results. What outcomes do you have now? That's what is happening on the inside.

Does it take effort to focus on the fulfillment of what you want? Yes. Do you have to be deliberate with your focus to create the outcomes you want? Yes, there is effort involved in navigating your focus and the state of your inner being.

But here's what I can tell you from my own experience and the thousands of people that have successfully manifested their outcomes with the 7-day manifestation experiment. You've got nothing to lose. If this doesn't work, you do the 7 days and nothing happens, you can always have your old life back. But if something happens to fall into your lap during those 7 days, something unexpected that highlights who you really are, it could change your life forever.

Join the conversation here:

"Open Camera App on your Phone to scan this QR
Code and watch the video now."

FREE RESOURCE:

I've created a guided meditation so that you can get past the analytical mind and into a deep trance so that you set and realize your intentions. It's called the Magic Manifestation Meditation and it's free.

You can download it here: www.magicmanifestation.ca

"Open Camera App on your Phone to scan this QR Code and download the meditation now."

Made in the USA
Las Vegas, NV
03 October 2022

56449464R00095